D'Dana George

4⁰⁰

fil

mer

7/20

OUT
OF THE
BLUE

THE **UNEXPECTED** ADVENTURE
OF LIFE **INTERRUPTED**

GREG MURTHA

O U T OF THE B L U E

Published by Clear Day Publishing, a division of Clear Day Media Group LLC, Waco, TX *{cleardaypublishing.com}*. Audio edition and ebook available wherever digital books are sold.

Published in association with Ivey Harrington Beckman, *{iveyharringtonbeckman.com}* and Derek Bell, Mosaic Strategy Group *{mosaicstrategy.us}*.

All Scripture passages are taken from Holy Bible, New International Version®, NIV® Copyright ©1973, 1978, 1984, 2011 by Biblica, Inc.® Used by permission. All rights reserved worldwide.

For foreign and subsidiary rights, contact dbell@mosaicstrategy.us.

ISBN: 978-0-9863734-8-0
Library of Congress Control Number: 2017947572
Cover Design: Jay Smith, JuiceBox Designs *{juiceboxdesigns.com}*
Interior Design: Lux Creative *{theluxcreative.com}*
Printed in the United States of America.

This book is dedicated to

Tracey and Jackson
What an adventure we have been on! Yay, God!

Kelli, Zac, Dad, and Vicki
Thank you for doing life with me.

Mom
You are an incredible woman through and through.

CONTENTS

PRAISE FOR
OUT OF THE BLUE

Watching Greg Murtha's journey from success to significance to surrender has been a great privilege. I'm grateful he wrote *Out of the Blue*. It holds much wisdom that should speak to the way we live. Please read this book and be inspired to live the great adventure God has designed for you.

> **BOB BUFORD**, *founder of Leadership Network and the Halftime Institute and author of* Halftime: Moving from Success to Significance

How many people do you know who embrace absolutely everything? Even cancer. When I met Greg Murtha, I realized I was gazing into the eyes of the person I wanted to become. Brave, intelligent, funny, confident, and faithful, Greg embraces a complete acceptance of his fate with pure joy and excitement. Knowing him is a beautiful gift. You, too, will feel that and be incredibly inspired after reading *Out of the Blue*.

> **SCOTT HAMILTON**, *Olympic Gold Medalist, Figure Skater Commentator and Cancer Survivor*

Greg Murtha is one remarkable person—engaging, authentic, a lover of life, and best of all, spiritually focused. Perhaps that's why God selected him for a unique journey with suffering that lets us glimpse the often-unnoticed opportunities swirling around us and the wonders they offer up when, like Greg, we're willing to step into them. Greg's book will inspire you. It certainly inspired me.

DR. ROBERT LEWIS, *Founder of Men's Fraternity*

In *Out of the Blue*, Greg has captured for us the deep wisdom that transformed him into one of the people I most admire on this planet.

LLOYD REEB, *Halftime Spokesman*

When faced with an out-of-the-blue moment, the kind where something totally unexpected interrupts and shakes your world, take a deep breath and reach for Greg Murtha's book. You will be inspired, encouraged, convicted, loved, and filled with hope —real, undeniable hope that speaks abundance and life into every situation, even the dire ones.

KAY WILLS WYMA, *blogger* and *author of* Cleaning House and I'm Happy for You (Sort of ... not really)

Reading *Out of the Blue* is a risky venture. If you take in Greg's message, your life will never be the same. Greg helps us understand the hurting, battered, and bruised people of the world—and how to be the hands and feet of Jesus to them (and we're all hurt, battered, and bruised). Thank you, Greg, for the gifts of your life and this book. You're the best friend a guy could ever have.

DEREK BELL, *President, The Mosaic Strategy Group*

Greg Murtha is a man after God's own heart. *Out of the Blue* will inspire you to embrace interruptions, listen to the Holy Spirit, and say, *yes*. It is when we say *yes*, as Greg has done, that God turns everyday life into an unexpected adventure.

KATIE DAVIS MAJORS, *author of* Kisses from Katie *and* Daring to Hope

Greg's purpose in life is to be a messenger of God, who loves us unconditionally. This love gives meaning to Greg's illness, and the message of *Out of the Blue* gives meaning to our lives.

KEVIN BAILEY AM, *Director, Parousia Media*

We read every word of *Out of the Blue*. What a gift! Greg, because of your faithfulness, we're going to be more aware, more interruptible, more focused on others, more vulnerable, more audibly prayerful with others, more scraped, bruised, and used up sliding into death— giving God alone the glory.

TODD AND ALEX WAGNER, *Watermark Community Church*

Out of the Blue is the deeply moving and compelling story of Greg Murtha's battle with cancer. But it's a book that is full of hope, joy, and a bold invitation to live for what matters most.

PETER GREER, *President and CEO, HOPE International and coauthor of* Mission Drift

This powerful book is a humbling and honest account of a great man whose life was interrupted by cancer. It's an affirming message of hope that traces the steps of Greg's journey to the foot of Calvary's cross. *Out of the Blue* is a great tool, especially if you are struggling with slowing down or finding the simplicity in loving and following Christ.

JOE WHITE, *Founder of Kanakuk Camps*

Greg Murtha has modeled what it means to live a life sold out to Jesus. His obvious love for his Savior in the face of great adversity has left an imprint on many lives.

BOB LEPINE, *Cohost of FamilyLife Today*

Greg has shown us all what it looks like to follow Christ and run the race of life all the way to the finish line. My life, like many others, has been sharpened, shaped, and enriched by knowing him.

DR. DENNIS RAINEY, *CEO of FamilyLife*

Out of the Blue does more than motivate you to "live like you were dying." It equips you with eternal truths for living with joy, spontaneity, and love whether you're in a season of health and prosperity or pain and frustration.

JEFF SPADAFORA, *Halftime Institute, Director of Global Coaching Services and author of* TheJoy-Model.com

If you've ever suffered, this is the book for you. If you've ever gotten so down with the struggles and obstacles life can throw your way, *Out of the Blue* will give perspective. As Greg Murtha journals his battle with Stage IV cancer, you'll count your blessings, put on visionary glasses, and determine to make an impact on this world before your time is up.

> **JT OLSON**, *Founder and Executive Director of Both Hands Foundation and author of* The Orphan, The Widow, and Me

Few people ever have the chance to know someone like Greg. His friendships and acts of service for others are legendary. I'm a better follower of Christ, husband, father, and friend because of Greg Murtha.

> **RAY GARY**, *CEO iDonate*

I have been incredibly blessed by knowing Greg and seeing firsthand the way he loves and encourages others—and the way he loves and encourages me. *Out of the Blue* is such a blessing. I am a richer person for having read it, and I believe you will be too.

> **HENRY KAESTNER**, *Managing Partner, Sovereign's Capital*

FOREWORD

BY BOB GOFF

I met Greg and his family in a restaurant in Washington, D.C., some years ago. We had a short time together, but it was an important one to me. What immediately impressed me was a guy who loved God and his family. You could see it from across the room. It was like it was in the air. What drew me to Greg and his family was what made men climb sycamore trees to get a better look at Jesus. It was why a woman pulled on Jesus' shirttails when he passed by. They wanted the same thing I did when I met Greg—to experience what it feels like to get inside of the blast radius of extravagant love.

You'll read in these pages about Greg's accomplishments, and there were many. But you won't care about any of them. Here's why. Greg didn't either. You see, this is a book about slowing down the pace of your busy life to find the peace of God for your tired soul. It's not a playbook about what Greg learned running successful organizations, but what he learned when he skidded to a stop at the feet of Jesus. Greg realized there is a big difference between what works and what lasts. It's a distinction he wants us to know too.

Out of the Blue is a long love letter penned by a guy who discovered God doesn't need our help, but he'll do whatever it takes to get our attention. Cancer landed Greg in the hospital, but understanding how much God delights in being with us led Greg home. Whether faith has been a big deal in your life or something which has felt distant, Greg's words are a simple wooden signpost pointing toward a carpenter from Nazareth. Greg left these ideas with us because he figured out what some of us are still discovering: We'll be known for our opinions, but we'll be remembered for our love. Greg will be remembered for his.

Our lives are a lot of ambiguity followed by an eternity full of certainty. Greg has a big advantage over us. What we are peeking through a knothole trying to understand, Greg sees completely. None of us knows why things happen to us and those we love. We probably won't fully understand most of these things until we are face to face with Jesus. What Greg figured out through his challenges is that God will use our brokenness because he knows he'll have more pieces to work with.

It took Beethoven seven years to complete his ninth symphony. When he wrote the last few notes, this great composer was deaf and couldn't hear it performed. Greg isn't with us in person any longer, but his spirit lives on in our hearts and the beautiful pages of this book. *Out of the Blue* is Greg's last symphony. Our lives are just a few pieces of sheet music. It's a guess, but I think Greg would want us to grab a kettledrum or a piccolo, a violin, or a couple of trash-can lids and make a joyful sound to God with our lives. He'd want us to play a song filled with redeemed pain and joy and grace and Jesus. I don't know what it will be like in heaven. Maybe we'll be watching what is happening in the lives of the people we love. Maybe not. I think Greg will be hoping we'll play songs pointing toward a loving God, and he'll be tapping his feet while we do.

If you were looking for a book lamenting the brevity of life, find another one. *Out of the Blue* is a party on many pages. Greg writes the way he lived, with depth in simplicity and with equal parts passion and purpose. His words are overflowing with joy and sincerity and anticipation.

This is a book about strength, not weakness. These are pages filled with hope, not despair. *Out of the Blue* is about Greg's life, not his death. What you're about to read is a celebration of what it looks like to be lowered through the roof to the feet of Jesus. But here's the thing: Greg isn't the guy on the stretcher; he's the guy on the roof with a couple of ropes around us.

Bob Goff

Dear God,

Thanks for loving us. Thank you so much for friends, for family, for people who love with every ounce of who they are, for people who embrace interruption as a gift, for people drawn according to your purposes. Just thank you.

I love you, God. I pray that everyone who reads this book will say, "Yes, Jesus! I'm all in!" It's that simple. Because when we get out of the way and trust you for the results, God, great things happen. Father, may every person say yes to the adventure of a lifetime that can change the world. And what an adventure it is to walk arm in arm and hand in hand with you, the Creator of the Universe. There is no better deal than that! So, whether I have two years left on Hotel Earth, two months, or two whatever, I'm in, God. I'm all in.

Greg
June 18, 2017
Vanderbilt University Medical Center

A NOTE FROM GREG

Interruption has taught me an amazing truth: When I focus on what God leads me to do, I get to play a role in the ultimate story—his story—and that's where I've found life. That's where the adventure begins.

IF MY LIFE HAD GONE AS PLANNED, I would be running full speed ahead: a 52-year-old Brooks Brothers-clad male with the world by the tail, a picture of physical and fiscal success. I would be at the top of my game, focusing most of my time and energy on exceeding the previous quarter's earnings. I would be attempting to follow Jesus my way, pushing myself hard to gain God's approval (and that of others) while gripped by the fear of never measuring up.

I would rather enjoy life this way (God's way) if only for a few years, than live for decades wrapped up in my small, timid plans and the insecurities present in that lifestyle.

But my life didn't go as planned. Not even close. Cancer interrupted it. And that's a good thing because, without cancer, I would never have embraced the joy of following Jesus with reckless abandon or experienced the exhilaration of sensing the promptings of the Holy Spirit. I would never have acted in obedience to what he leads me to do (what he has wired me to do) or joined him in his master plan.

> Without cancer, I would have remained that somber, self-righteous, smug, narrow-minded Christian who turns people off.

In God's grace, he allowed me to get so sick I had to slow down, abandon my plans, move out of the way, and learn to trust him by just being. Frankly, I would rather enjoy life this way (God's way) if only for a few years, than live for decades wrapped up in my small, timid plans and the insecurities present in that lifestyle. You might say, cancer got me out of my performance-based, fearful existence and into the bigger story: the grand adventure. Sheldon Vanauken, the author of *A Severe Mercy*, understood the difference because he lived it.

> *The best argument for Christianity is Christians: their joy, their certainty, their completeness. But the strongest argument against Christianity is also Christians— when they are somber and joyless, when*

they are self-righteous and smug in com-
placent consecration, when they are nar-
row and repressive, then Christianity dies a
thousand deaths.[1]

Without cancer, I would have remained that somber, self-righteous, smug, narrow-minded Christian who turns people off: the Christian who judges instead of loves, clings tightly to the status-quo plan, and thinks he can earn God's approval. The Christian who misses the joy of simply following Jesus the way he intended.

Now, I understand Jesus' words in Matthew 11:28-30:

Come to me, all you who are weary and
burdened, and I will give you rest. Take my
yoke upon you and learn from me, for I am
gentle and humble in heart, and you will
find rest for your souls. For my yoke is easy
and my burden is light.

Before cancer, his yoke was hard, and his burden was heavy because I, unintentionally, made it that way.

It's quite ironic that writing a book was never on my long, well-planned to-do list. But God prompted me—a man with a weak heart, Stage IV cancer, and the attention span of a goldfish—to put into words what suffering has taught me. And while I'm physically weaker than ever, I've never been more alive. It's my hope and prayer that *Out of the Blue* will help you embrace interruption as an adventure, rather than adversity. Following Jesus in the unexpected has led me to life-giving exploits. I want the same for you because lots of things interrupt our well-planned lives. Small things. Big things. In-between things.

Out of the Blue is not a what-happened-next book. It's a blend of wisdom unearthed from Cancer Road paired with a collection of Facebook blog posts that, to my surprise, have deeply resonated with people over the past five years. At the end of each chapter, you'll find excerpts from those posts that speak to the heart of the matter. Nothing flashy. Just me being vulnerable. *Out of the Blue* was birthed from my Facebook posts, which stuns me, to be frank.

But *Out of the Blue* isn't about me, not really, because the world doesn't revolve around me. For years, I thought it did. And I lived that way. Before my cancer diagnosis on January 27, 2012, I was just writing my small story. Out-of-the-blue interruption has taught me when I focus on what God leads me to do, I get to play a pivotal role in the ultimate story—his story—and that's where I've found life.

That's where the adventure begins.

My challenge for those who read this short book is quite simple:

- Celebrate every day you have on earth,
- view interruptions as opportunities to play a role in God's ultimate story,
- and do what God prompts you to do.

I could quote Jesus or the Apostle Paul at this point; however, I feel compelled to go with Hunter S. Thompson because his words express exactly how I feel.

Life should not be a journey to the grave with the intention of arriving safely in a pretty and well-preserved body, but rather to skid in broadside in a cloud of smoke, thoroughly used up, totally worn out, and loudly proclaiming, 'Wow!'[2]

Will you join me in the great broadside skid?

LIFE INTERRUPTED

BAD THINGS CAN TURN OUT
TO BE GOOD THINGS—
REALLY GOOD THINGS.

ON A COLD DECEMBER MORNING IN 2011, I ran eleven miles on the picturesque Crocket Hills Trail in Middle Tennessee. There, trees form a canopy over the path, a stream flows quietly nearby, and it's not uncommon to see deer, turkeys, raccoons, and squirrels living the life—blissfully unaffected by biking or running humans. That morning, I was in the zone. With a powerful but loose stride, I clipped off the miles, one by one, breathing in crisp, clean air and feeling good.

As a 46-year-old man in what I thought was peak physical condition, eleven miles was nothing. Afterward, sweating but pumped, I headed for the bathroom at the YMCA. That's when my runner's high deflated. It appeared as if someone had poured a container of bright-red blood into the toilet. It was a lot of blood, and I realized instantly, *this is not good.*

From the outside looking in, I had it made. As the Chief Connections Officer at the Halftime Institute, I recruited high-profile people from around the world for an organization I cofounded with Bob Buford, whose groundbreaking book *Halftime: Moving from Success to Significance* inspired many to make that move. My beautiful wife, Tracey, and I lived in upscale Brentwood, Tennessee, with our young son, Jackson.

Before moving to Brentwood, we were founding members of Watermark Community Church in Dallas, where we spearheaded the follow-up ministry and led two small groups. An immigrant family of four from Zimbabwe, Africa, lived with us. Neighbors viewed us as wonderful humanitarians. Church friends enjoyed doing life with us.

> Five words changed everything: "Mr. Murtha, you have cancer."

But then, five words changed everything:

"Mr. Murtha, you have cancer."

On January 27, 2012, one month after that scenic eleven-mile run, Tracey and I left the doctor's office and headed to our favorite Nashville eatery, Calypso Café. We were seated at a table for two in the middle of the well-liked restaurant. Laughter and easy-going banter wafted from other tables.

After the server had taken our order, I looked at Tracey and mumbled, "The doctor just said I have cancer," which was both a statement and a question.

"Yes," Tracey slowly replied. "He did."

Tears started streaming down my face. While I wasn't sure what the future held, I was certain nothing would ever be the same. Out of the blue, my well-planned life had been radically interrupted.

WAITING FOR THE CALL

Frankly, my glass is not half full or half empty. My glass is overflowing. I once took a personality assessment at a corporate retreat. The individual who administered the assessment told me he had never met anyone who scored as high as I did in the realm of optimistic extroversion. Heck, I was a cheerleader in college; positive thinking is in my DNA. So, even though my cancer diagnosis brought me to tears in the middle of Calypso Café, I immediately believed, deep down, we would beat it. I had no idea what beating it would look like, how it would feel, or even what it would require of me, but I was confident we would win.

Days later, after we had chosen a surgeon and set a date for my operation, I made a cancer battle plan. I was good with planning and had a long to-do list to prove it. Although I was already in the best shape of my adult life, I decided to train for the surgery. I upped my running, biking, and weightlifting to the next level. It was my way of saying, *Bring it on! Want a fight? You've got it!*

On a Friday at the crack of dawn, I arrived at the hospital for my operation. Dr. Paul Wise and his surgical team removed one foot of my colon laparoscopically. On Saturday, guests filled my hospital room, and I felt great. Sunday, I walked the 18th-of-a-mile-loop on my floor—18 times.

On Monday, I walked out of the hospital carrying my bag. Tuesday evening, Tracey and I attended a fundraiser for colorectal cancer awareness at the Country Music Hall of Fame, an invitation we had accepted long before my diagnosis. (My mother died of complications from the disease.) While there, we ran into Dr. Wise, a few of my nurses, and my oncologist. They were amazed we were out and about already, but I felt terrific.

For the remainder of the week, I rested at home and waited for the call about my lab results. Candidly, I was cautiously optimistic the cancer that had interrupted my well-planned life was behind me. Thursday afternoon, I was sitting on the leather sofa in our family room when my cell phone rang. Dr. Wise got straight to the point.

"Mr. Murtha, the results are in, and we're dealing with Aggressive Stage III cancer. The tumor has grown through the colon wall, and there is evidence of cancer cells in your lymphatic system. Typically, I encourage my patients to wait a few weeks to heal from surgery before we start chemotherapy; however, I recommend that you start chemo immediately."

I'm not certain what else Dr. Wise said that day because I was stunned when I heard words that were not in my plan, words that were the direct opposite of what family and friends were praying.

Hearing "Aggressive Stage III cancer" felt like a hard kick to my gut, and I simply tried to hold myself together until the conversation ended. I knew Aggressive Stage III was the wicked stuff. The kind of cancer that is excruciatingly unkind. The kind that kills. Fast.

I knew Aggressive Stage III was the wicked stuff. The kind of cancer that is excruciatingly unkind. The kind that kills. Fast.

I sat on our leather sofa with tears rolling down my face. The echo of ugly sobs filled the silence.

I wondered, *How will I tell Tracey? How do I explain this to my 10-year-old son?*

A CHANGE OF HEART

Today, five years after that gut-check phone call from Dr. Wise, I'm not the picture of physical health I once was. Walk with me, and you'll hear a cough rattle in my chest where cancer cells now coat my lungs. Peek at an MRI of my heart, and you'll see stents, byproducts of two out-of-the-blue heart attacks that left me with a heart limited to 60 percent capacity. (Eleven-mile runs are a thing of the past.) Doctors have now reclassified my Aggressive Stage III cancer as Stage IV. (Typically, Stage IV colon cancer that has metastasized to the lungs comes with a two-year expiration date, so my family and I believe we're ahead of the curve, and possibly living on borrowed time.)

But don't feel sorry for me. Strange as it sounds, I view cancer as a gift. I thank God for it because it means I'm not the man I used to be. Sure, this interruption to my well-planned life was jarring. And chemo is hell. But I'm thankful for cancer because it has given me the ability to focus on what matters.

For years, I would strategically develop a plan and then operate against the plan, ruthlessly avoiding interruptions. And I had big plans for 2012 and beyond. In high-octane Murtha mode, doing stuff for

> For years, I would strategically develop a plan and then operate against the plan, ruthlessly avoiding interruptions.

God was the way to go—and I was good at it. (At least that's what others said and what I kept telling myself.)

There's nothing wrong with having a plan. My problem? Performance. This behavior was an effort, on my part, to please my Heavenly Father, to win his approval. I was target-locked on implementing a strategy instead of listening for God's promptings. I was working my plan, not his.

Bob Goff, the author of *Love Does*, got it right when he tweeted, "God's more interested in our hearts than our plans."[3] God radically changed my plans, but the worst diagnosis is the best thing that ever happened to me because it changed my heart. In the past, I marched to the tune of my to-do list because I was afraid of not measuring up. Afraid of not having what it took. Afraid I would fail. Afraid I would not please God. Before cancer, I avoided speaking in public because I believed I wasn't worthy—and I thought I had nothing to say.

> God radically changed my plans, but the worst diagnosis is the best thing that ever happened to me because it changed my heart.

After enduring multiple surgeries, two heart attacks, and 75 rounds of chemo (an unofficial *Guinness Book of World Records* milestone), I now have something worth saying because it's God's message, not mine. Cancer has given me a different perspective, a voice, and a clear understanding of how to join God in his plan instead of focusing on implementing mine.

You see, bad things can turn out to be good things—really good things.

I'M ALL IN

Soon after my diagnosis, while I once again sat on the leather sofa in our family room, I made a commitment: *God, whatever you want me to do, the answer is yes. I'm all in.* I committed to living an authentic, vulnerable, filter-free life of what you see is what you get—the good, the bad, and the ugly— and I committed to sharing this with others. Did I take a deep, somewhat shaky breath when contemplating the untraveled road ahead? Sure. Did I trust God to show me the way? Absolutely.

Basic economics says when something is in short supply, its value increases. This axiom applies to life as well. For me, days are more precious. Life is short; it disappears as quickly as the visible mist of sprayed cologne. The time God has given me is treasured, and I'm much more intentional than I've ever been about where I invest it because it's my most valued asset. In the midst, I've discovered what brings me life. Out-of-the-blue interruptions teach you stuff like this.

These days, I spend a lot of time sitting in a chemo chair, and people who are battling for their lives surround me. Personally, I refer to dying as moving to the front of the line, and I'm at peace with that. Now, even as I struggle to breathe deeply, I'm comfortable with the full breath of who God created me to be.

I'm comfortable with the full breath of who God created me to be. I realize I'm not what I do, what I produce or earn, or even who I know. I don't have to perform or impress. In his infinite wisdom, God interrupted me, deleted my to-do list, and changed my elaborate plans to his simple one:

> *Listen to my still, small voice, Greg, and do what I ask. Be the hands, feet, and heart of Jesus to those you meet in the chemo infusion room, grocery store, parking garage, your neighborhood—or wherever I lead you.*

April 9, 2012
More Like Him

Today is round two of chemotherapy. While I'm not looking forward to the infusion and to carrying the pump for 48 hours, I'm thankful God would choose me to suffer. I pray he will allow me to be an encouragement to my oncologist, my medical caregivers, and my fellow cancer patients.

Help me, Jesus, to be a light in what can or could be a dark place.

It's more natural for me to look to Jesus whenever I'm afraid, in pain, or have a need. When things are perfect, it's easy to forget my need and utter dependence on him. When I'm feeling poorly, Jesus is constantly on my mind. I have a feeling he'll be on my mind a lot this week.

While I wouldn't choose cancer, it has been a gift. As a result:

1. My conversations have been deeper with everyone—from my son, Jackson, to Tracey, to friends, neighbors, even strangers.
2. I'm living more intentionally as I realize that all our days are numbered. We're not even promised tomorrow.
3. I'm taking long walks and spending much more time in prayer with Tracey. She and I are making long-term financial decisions that moving forward will free us up to live, give, and serve.

As a result, while I ask you to pray I will be healed and the chemotherapy will destroy the rogue cancer cells, I want you also to pray Jesus will work in me through the queasiness and nausea to make me more like him.

May 2, 2012
The Simplicity of His Love for Us

Thursday, January 26, I received a terrible report that my friend Clark Millspaugh has cancer. To fully connect with him, I promptly went out the next day and got my cancer diagnosis.

Clark has been the president & CEO of two oil & gas exploration companies in Tulsa. He is a terrific father, husband, and friend. He has taken his skills and abilities and led other men through *Wild at Heart* adventures. Clark spearheaded Men's Fraternity in his community. He partnered with an urban elementary school and established a grocery store for the poor. He launched a 24/7 prayer room. He created a global garden and arranged a mobile healthcare clinic to provide services for the poor in his community on a biweekly basis. Heck, we even included a video of him on *Halftime. org*. So, to say Clark's recent journal entry blew me away is an understatement.

Frankly, I shouldn't be surprised because I'm learning in our suffering Jesus really shows up, and, goodness, has Clark suffered. He had seven weeks of chemo in a row to prepare for an upcoming bone marrow transplant. His level of suffering has been far deeper than what I've had to endure thus far, and based on what he shared, his level of understanding is deeper as well.

With what I just shared as a backdrop, allow me to encourage you to read Clark's journal entry:

> *God has been so gracious and faithful throughout this journey, and I know he will be until it's complete. God has been at work on my heart and soul.*
>
> *"Be still and know that I'm God" has taken on a new dimension.*

Performance, busyness, striving, control, pride, success, idolatry, and planning have all taken such a foothold in my life that it's taken these seven weeks for me to recognize my need for repentance and to seek forgiveness from those I love.

It's going to mean a new life of resting in Jesus. I've missed the rest and intimacy.

Not many people would string that confession together: *performance, busyness, striving, control, pride, success, idolatry, planning.* However, I'm certain, if we were truly honest, we would all say a hearty *amen* that we, too, suffer from the same list of afflictions.

Interesting that God would allow us to be stricken with a horrible disease to enable us to understand the simplicity of his love for us. He doesn't require us to jump through endless religious hoops. He, on the contrary, desires for us to sit on his lap, look him in the eye, and say "thank you."

Thank you, God, for loving me enough to

allow me to suffer. Thank you for opening my eyes to the crazy sin of performance. Thank you for allowing me to experience life through serving others. Thank you for being the God of love who so wants to have an intimate relationship with me. Just thank you.

So, what does this have to do with you?

1. *What was the last out-of-the-blue interruption to your life?*
2. *What would you do if you received a life-threatening diagnosis?*
3. *Are you that somber, self-righteous, smug, narrow-minded Christian who turns people off? The Christian who judges others instead of loving them, clings tightly to the status-quo plan, and thinks he can earn God's approval? The Christian who misses the joy of simply following Jesus the way he intended?*

IN THE
PANIC SEAT

OUR UTMOST SOURCE OF
SERVICE SPRINGS FROM OUR
GREATEST WEAKNESS, THE
PLACE OF OUR DEEPEST PAIN.

EVERYTHING IN ME SCREAMED, *GET OFF THIS PLANE!* It was a hot, sticky August morning in Dallas. I was seated in the back of Southwest Flight 2Y, headed to Little Rock. When the pilot had made his final announcements, taxied to the end of the runway, and hit the throttle, I had broken out in a sweat. My seatbelt felt like a straight-jacket. My shoes strangled my feet. My belt felt three sizes too small. As I gasped for breath, I wondered, *am I having a heart attack?*

That's when a total stranger reached across the aisle, grabbed my arm, looked me in the eyes, and said, "You're going to be ok. You're having a panic attack. Lean back, close your eyes, take deep breaths, and I'll talk to you once we get to cruising altitude."

After the plane had leveled off, my new friend introduced himself. He was a husband, father, businessman, and church deacon who wrestled with panic attacks. A traumatic family experience had triggered them. Intruders invaded his home, duct-taped him to a chair, and abducted his wife and daughter. He was powerless to help them. Since that day, he has wrestled with low-level anxiety, panic attacks, and a sense of not being in control.

To say I was thankful for his presence on that flight is an understatement. Candidly, he was God sent. I'm not sure what I would have done if he hadn't been there. He recognized what I was going through—and rather than ignore me or call for the flight attendant—he engaged. His "been there" explanation of what was going on with me, along with his reassurance I wasn't having a heart attack

> Often, the place where we've suffered is where we have the most to give.

or going crazy, gave me the confidence I would exit Southwest Flight 2Y in Little Rock without the aid of paramedics.

I believe our utmost source of service springs from our greatest weakness, the place of our deepest pain. Often, the place where we've suffered is where we have the most to give. That man's response to my panic attack is a prime example of engaging the adventure of an interruption from the place of deepest pain. It's monumental to say to someone who's struggling, "I've been there, and you're not crazy." It requires no small amount of attentiveness. However, when we embrace interruptions with vulnerability, God gets the credit—and we get out of the way.

NOT MEASURING UP

The purpose of that trip to Little Rock on that sultry August day in 2001 was to gain the input of Robert Lewis (my friend and mentor) for my new role as president of the Halftime Institute. The

Halftime board encouraged me to take the position because I was already fulfilling most of the duties. Deep inside, I knew the position wasn't the best fit for me; however, I thought I could serve just as well as the next guy—and it was cool to have a business card with the title *President* printed on it.

The Halftime Institute was a young organization with opportunity at every turn. After people had read Bob Buford's book, *Halftime: Moving from Success to Significance,* they would either call or show up at Bob's office and ask, "How do I make the move?"

Our team developed an organization that provided a university of sorts for the second half of life. It was an energizing environment that brought together some of the smartest people I had ever been around. It wasn't uncommon for me to share a table with Peter Drucker, Bob Buford, Ken Blanchard, and a circle of Harvard MBAs. I would often hear a little voice inside my head ask, *Greg, what in the heck are you doing here?* My inferiority complex came from the fact I was a 33-year-old man with a public-school education from the state of Arkansas, where our motto for public school

> I would often hear a little voice inside my head ask, *Greg, what in the heck are you doing here?*

education is, "Thank God for Mississippi."

The nagging feeling of not measuring up, not having what it took, always gripped me. I masked these emotions by taking on more responsibilities and keeping busy in meetings when I felt anxiety spiking. Whenever Bob asked me to take on a project, my emphatic response was, "Consider it done."

But inside I was a mess. Inside, I was dying a slow death. During the time in my life when I should have celebrated the ultimate sense of accomplishment with nothing to fear, I felt terror.

Early in life, I learned to perform to gain my father's approval. And perform I did: from getting the lead in the school play to becoming captain of the baseball team to recruiting a band that won numerous talent shows. Most everything I did was an attempt to please my father, who, as a young, inexperienced dad, made a few parenting miscalculations—as all of us do. (He only wanted the best for me and pushed me hard toward excellence. Dad learned a lot about parenting along the way, and I often tap his deep well of "been there" wisdom as I parent my son. I once told Jackson, "Just because I'm a parent doesn't mean I know everything. You didn't come with an owner's manual." To which my son replied, "I totally agree, Dad.")

Unwittingly, I transferred the performance habit to my relationship with God. Everything I did was an attempt to please God, to get his approval, to make myself worthy.

The church of my youth didn't help matters. It didn't teach grace or that God loves us just the way we are. Nope, it taught sin management. Faith was a list of rules: don't smoke, don't drink, don't dance, don't *whatever*. (To be candid, I sucked at sin management. I often felt guilty, and my mentality during my first couple of years in college was, *If I'm going to feel this guilty for drinking a beer, I might as well drink 12.*)

The church of my youth didn't help matters. It didn't teach grace or that God loves us just the way we are. Nope, it taught sin management.

I was a study in contrasts back then. When I wasn't completing pledging duties at the fraternity, I was attending faith-based meetings. Monday night was Campus Crusade; Tuesday was Fellowship of Christian Athletes; Wednesday was Student Mobilization. Deep inside, I was searching for something real. I was looking for answers, for ways to please God. I didn't find them in Christian activities, but I kept looking. My ongoing attempt to please God stuck with me post college and into my career. In fact, the habit escalated over the years.

NO MORE

The final performance straw that broke me landed on a Tuesday morning, not long after that panic-filled Southwest flight. I had gone for my morning run and returned home to have a quiet time before heading to the Halftime office. For several months, a Zimbabwean family of four (Dave, Amber, and their children, Robbie and Sarah) lived with us, which meant constant activity. That Tuesday morning was no different.

After grabbing a cup of coffee, along with my journal and Bible, I sat down just as Amber scurried through our family room with Sarah and Robbie in tow. As she passed the sofa, Amber said, "Greg, I'm running late. Could you stop what you're doing and pray for the kids?"

Up until that second, I had said *yes* to everything asked of me.

Would I serve as president for Halftime? *Against my better judgment, I said yes.*

Would I lead a small group? *If one is good, then two must be better. I said yes to both.*

Would I lead the Watermark follow-up ministry, administration and all? *Sure. (Even though, if pressed, I would have a tough time administrating myself out of a wet paper bag.)*

Would we house a family of four from Zimbabwe? *Why not?*

The moment Amber asked me to stop what I was doing and pray for her children, I knew something was wrong.

I didn't respond to her request.

Instead, I started sobbing. Big, gulping sobs.

No, I thought, *I cannot take on one more responsibility*.

No, I cannot do one more thing. No. No. No.

My out-of-the-blue reaction cleared the room—fast. Feeling a bit stunned, I steamed my brain in the shower and headed to work. Upon arrival, I took the stairs. For some reason, I was afraid to get on the elevator. Too confining. When I entered my office, I was physically unable to look at the whiteboard, where 15 ongoing initiatives were listed. Looking at them made me feel lightheaded, so I asked two administrators from our team to make notes from the whiteboard—and erase it.

After making a quick U-turn back down the stairs, I called my doctor to say I was on my way—work me in—fast. My blood pressure was through the roof, but other than stress, there was no reason for the spike. That reality eventually led me to Dr. Joan Faubion, a Christian psychologist who specializes in

My first thought? *It's over. When I tell Bob Buford what I'm experiencing, he'll replace me with someone who can handle the pressure.*

helping overachievers recover from crashes caused by dysfunction. After our first conversation, she encouraged me to drop everything for three weeks of intensive, outpatient therapy.

How in the heck am I supposed to do that? I wondered.

Reading my mind, Dr. Faubion leaned forward, looked me in the eyes, and with a soft but firm voice said, "Greg, your elevator never goes below the second floor. While what you're engaged in—running, quiet times—should provide the respite and regeneration you need, your brain is always racing. I want to teach you to relax and rest."

My first thought? *It's over. When I tell Bob Buford what I'm experiencing, he'll replace me with someone who can handle the pressure.*

To my surprise, Bob said, "Greg, you're in good company. Rick Warren[4] and Bill Hybels[5] wrestle with anxiety and panic attacks. Get help. We'll be here when you return."

Even though Dr. Faubion helped me, I must be frank. I didn't learn to relax and rest until my cancer diagnosis. It was then I was forced to slow down because I physically *couldn't* run anymore.

Couldn't juggle multiple projects.

Couldn't say, "Consider it done."

Yes, the panic attack I had on Southwest Flight 2Y in 2001—followed by meltdowns at my home and the office—reflected a culmination of years of playing a role and operating from my skill-set mix to win the approval and applause of men. As terrifying as that time of life was, it marked the beginning of a long and, at times, a fear-filled road to discover who I was and how I could live at peace, enjoy slowing down, and learn how God wanted to use me to help others.

July 7, 2012
Be Still and Know

Yesterday, I was sitting on the leather sofa in our family room, reading and enjoying a slow Saturday morning, when Jackson came bursting through the back door with the first of three requests.

"Dad, come watch me! I learned to dive off the diving board!"

I walked to the back deck, where I had a clear view of the pool. Jackson raced to the diving board and, sure enough, he dove in. It wasn't the best dive I've ever seen, but it was a dive nonetheless.

"Good job, buddy!" I yelled. With the thumbs up sign, I went back to the couch.

A few minutes later, Jackson came through the back door with another request.

"Dad, come watch me! Really! Come watch! I learned to do a backflip on the trampoline!"

I went out on the back deck to a place where I had a terrific view of the trampoline. Jackson climbed on, and sure enough, he did a backflip.

"Great job, Jackson! Seriously! I'm proud of you!"

Not ten minutes later Jackson raced into our home with yet another request.

"Dad, come watch me! I've learned to drift on the Go Kart!"
(Drifting is when you get going fast enough on a Go Kart, and you turn, sliding sideways before straightening out again.)

For those of you keeping score, Jackson had demonstrated a dive, a backflip, and drifting all within a 30-minute time frame.

Frankly, I love that Jackson wants my approval; however, he has it already. He's my only child, and I love him deeply. He doesn't have to perform to earn my love, acceptance, or approval.

This morning Jackson woke up with a 100-plus fever. He's listless and will not be going to school today. Since I work from home, Jackson has nestled next to me on the sofa with his head on my lap.

While I love that Jackson is mastering boy-hood skills, nothing brings me greater joy than to have him next to me with his head on my lap. As I run my fingers through his hair, while praying he feels better soon, another truth hits me.

God does not need us to perform for him. He is pleased when we slow down enough to put our heads on his lap. He doesn't need us to make grandiose plans to earn his love. He doesn't need us to earn his pleasure. We are his beloved. He loves us just the way we are, just as I love my boy.

How about we slow down and place our heads on our Heavenly Father's lap? It will bring God great joy.

"He says, 'Be still, and know that I am God; I will be exalted among the nations, I will be exalted in the earth.'" Psalm 46:10

February 9, 2016
What is the Source of Your Greatest Pain?

Recently I had the privilege of being served by a wonderful woman. For the life of me, I cannot remember her name; however, I will never forget her story. She served as my nurse, and she was responsible for administering my chemotherapy. As I often do, I asked her where she was from. She had recently moved from Northern California, where she lived in a small town in the Russian River Valley. She was a nurse there and had made the decision to make a significant change in her life.

She bragged on her son, an attorney in Manhattan, and her daughter, who is an incredibly compassionate wife and mother. Both volunteer at the Ronald McDonald House and engage with charities that support cancer patients.

Sensing there was more to the story, I asked, "To what do you attribute your kids' interest in serving in this capacity? She replied, "Her name was Briana, and she was my daughter and their sister."

Over a decade ago Briana, at 13 years of age, was diagnosed with inoperable brain cancer. She was a stellar young lady, who, when asked what her family could do for her, said, I want YOU to be happy, so I believe we should do something for my siblings.

My new friend shared that the greatest gifts her daughter had were faith and peace. She had complete trust in the love of Jesus. Briana knew she would be with

Jesus after she took her last breath, so she was more concerned about her family than herself.

Their family did not live close to a hospital, so the staff equipped my nurse, who was then a squeamish stay-at-home mom, with the tools she needed to care for her daughter. On numerous occasions, Briana would say, "Mom, you're good at this. You should consider becoming a nurse."

Following Briana's death, the marriage broke apart, as do many marriages hit by the loss of a child. My nurse chose to take her daughter's advice and go to nursing school. This choice provided a safe place to grieve in anonymity and to work on a skill she could use to serve others.

It's interesting the number of people who choose to serve in their area of greatest pain. Candidly, this is where a lot of us are most equipped to give back. The place where we've suffered is often the place where we have the most to give.

- *The recovering alcoholic who serves as a sponsor at AA*

- *The abused child who grows up to be a counselor*
- *The couple who overcame a bad marriage and now leads the marriage ministry at church*
- *The neglected child who becomes the involved teacher*
- *The kid who got picked on who advocates for students as a principal*
- *The mom who lost her teenaged daughter to cancer returns to serve others who are suffering from this disease*

Frankly, this is biblical stuff.

> *Praise be to the God and Father of our Lord Jesus Christ, the Father of compassion and the God of all comfort, who comforts us in all our troubles, so that we can comfort those in any trouble with the comfort we ourselves receive from God. For just as we share abundantly in the sufferings of Christ, so also our comfort abounds through Christ.*
> *2 Corinthians 1:3-5*

Yes, we find life whenever we take something difficult and give it to God. When we take our eyes off ourselves and focus on helping others, the knowledge gleaned from suffering becomes a healing balm. Yes, my nurse did an excellent job with me. She had compassion, skill, and knowledge attained through firsthand experience and suffering.

Where can you serve? What do you have to offer? We all have something, and we all benefit when just one more human dives in and offers his or her passion birthed in pain in service to others.

So, what does this have to do with you?

1. *When have you heard the voice of doubt question whether you have what it takes?*
2. *What is your greatest point of suffering, and how can that hurt be used to help someone else?*
3. *What would it take for you to be vulnerable enough to share your pain with someone?*

I NEVER SAW SICK PEOPLE

IF IT HADN'T BEEN FOR
CANCER, I WOULD HAVE
NEVER MADE THE DISCOVERY
THAT WE FIND LIFE WHEN WE
GIVE, NOT GET. AND I DON'T
MEAN STUFF. I MEAN
OURSELVES–OUR TIME.

AT AGE 46 I HAD A BIG BLIND SPOT—and a hearing problem. You see, I focused on me, on my next personal goal. I never even saw sick or hurting people. They were not blips on my radar screen; they were invisible. I ran right by them to get to my next goal.

For years, God had been nudging me to slow down, but I didn't listen. I didn't hear the still, small voice of the Holy Spirit continually saying, "Be still, Greg. Be still." Instead, I kept going. I was determined to execute plans to accomplish stuff for God—at work, church, and beyond. Long story short, I embraced the performing way of the world.

> "The performing way of the world is about impressing people, about creating your own parade of accomplishments." Ann Voskamp

Ann Voskamp, author of *The Broken Way*, puts it this way: "The performing way of the world is about impressing people, about creating your own parade of accomplishments."[6]

If I'm completely sincere, I wanted both. I wanted others to see me as an accomplished professional and a godly leader. As a result, I got neither. Time and time again, God sent me warning flares to slow down. However, without something forcing me to stop completely, I couldn't shift into a lower gear. I was addicted to accomplishment. I didn't have a lower gear.

So, God yanked my feet out from under me— ASICS® running shoes and all. Trust me; cancer is one heck of a speed bump. Cancer didn't merely slow me down; it stopped me cold. My butt is now planted in a chemo infusion chair every other week and will be for the rest of my life. After getting a large dose of toxic drugs, I spend at least three days just trying to recoup from the chemical beating. Due to neuropathy, a side effect of chemo, I can no longer feel the bottoms of my feet. Combine that with cancer that has metastasized to my lungs, giving me a persistent cough, and I can't run any-where, except to the bathroom.

But, man, has cancer improved my vision and hearing. I now see sick and hurting people. And the still, small voice of the Holy Spirit? Well, let's just say the deaf now hear. I have cancer to thank for that healing.

MAKING EYE CONTACT WITH GOD

For the past five years, I've been hanging around people with problems. They are fascinating indi-viduals. Before my diagnosis, I would have viewed them as frustrating interruptions, at best. At worst, I would have completely ignored them. I've met people wrestling with all forms of cancer, heart issues, and alcoholism, as well as a convict and a lung transplant recipient, just to name a few. If my life hadn't been interrupted by a life-threatening illness, I would have never made the discovery that we find life when we give, not get. And I don't mean stuff. I mean ourselves—our time.

When I finally made this discovery, I reflected on Jesus, his life, and how often people interrupted him. Those many interruptions allowed Jesus the opportunity to model what being his hands and feet looks like.

Jesus' mother, Mary, interrupted him at a wedding and asked him to solve a wine shortage. A royal guy from Capernaum, whose son was gravely ill, interrupted Jesus and requested a miraculous healing. An invalid in Bethesda interrupted Jesus about a dip in the pool. These are just the interruptions covered in the first four chapters of the Gospel of John. The list goes on and on.

Why was Jesus so open to interruptions? Why wasn't he more driven, like me, to accomplish goals? (After all, he was working under a rather tight time deadline.) The answer is quite simple.

> When people are sick, wounded, or needy, they are most open to conversations about faith. They slow down enough to make eye contact with God.

When people are sick, wounded, or needy, they are most open to conversations about faith. They slow down enough to make eye contact with God.

The adage, "There are no atheists in foxholes," applies to infusion rooms and oncology wings as well. There, you mostly find fragile, fearful people with a deep longing for healing, people who need a friend.

Early in my cancer journey, Kim Mordecai, a friend and cancer survivor, encouraged me to look for individuals in hospitals and waiting rooms and see them as God-orchestrated connections. She told me it was not an accident I was sick, and people would benefit from a fellow patient with interest in their well-being.

Kim got it right. She has been there. She has lived it. Cancer interrupted her life, and she saw the opportunities it created for connection and made the most of them.

Since my cancer diagnosis, the Holy Spirit has nudged me to encourage and pray for people in Nashville's Vanderbilt University Medical Center, Texas Oncology at Baylor in Dallas, and Houston's MD Anderson. Never once has anyone refused my offer of prayer.

> Cancer builds bridges and breaks down walls. You see suffering has an upside. It draws us to each other–and to God.

Cancer builds bridges and breaks down walls.

You see suffering has an upside. It draws us to each other—and to God. J. C. Ryle, the Bishop of Liverpool (Anglican Church) in the 1800's, understood this. He endured the loss of the family fortune, an illness that assaulted his large frame, and the chronic illnesses and deaths of two wives. Rather than take the stance of "curse God and die,"[7] Ryle embraced the abundance of suffering.

> *Let us mark this well. There is nothing which shows our ignorance so much as our impatience under trouble. We forget that every trial is a message from God—and intended to do us good in the end.*
>
> *Trials are intended . . .*
> *to make us think,*
> *to wean us from the world,*
> *to send us to the Bible,*
> *to drive us to our knees.*
>
> *Health is a good thing. But sickness is far better, if it leads us to God.*
>
> *Prosperity is a great mercy. But adversity is a greater one, if it brings us to Christ.*[8]

TIME TO MAKE A DIFFERENCE

Each chemo infusion appointment requires waiting in a designated room filled with fellow patients. They sit with loved ones, trying to make it through the day, hoping and praying for good news.

On treatment weeks, I'm fourteen days past my previous infusion, the longest reprieve from chemo I'm allowed. I'm finally feeling better, but the next beating is coming. While in the clinic, I pray God will make it clear to me the individual I should encourage and pray with. It truly is a "seek, and you will find" adventure.

One day, upon entering a room for lab work, I immediately spotted a man in his early 50s wearing flannel pajama bottoms. To obscure the massive tumor protruding from his head, he had wrapped gauze around it. His wife was sitting next to him. She had dark circles under her eyes and appeared to be hanging in there. Barely.

I sat down next to him and said, "Hi, I'm Greg." Soon afterward, the man was called back to have his blood drawn, and I asked his wife how she was doing. She replied, "Ok." To build camaraderie, I shared that my 65th round of chemotherapy was minutes away. We exchanged knowing smiles.

She and the man she loves are dealing with harsh realities. He's receiving radiation and chemotherapy. With the protruding tumor, he's hard to look at, and I'm certain most people just turn away.

In the real world, people shun those with protruding tumors, ashen faces, bald heads, and surgical masks. Sure, people stare and wonder, but they never truly see. I know because I didn't.

But behind those medical symbols are fascinating people brimming with hopes, dreams, and fears. When approached, I've discovered they are pleased to engage in conversation and often are wide open for prayer and kind words.

In the summer of 2016, my oncologist prescribed a new chemo drug for me, Panitumumab. (Candidly, I rarely refer to chemotherapy as a drug. Instead, I call it what it is: poison.) To that point on my cancer journey, I had been enduring chemo treatments that made me tired and nauseated, but I didn't look like a cancer patient. When I entered an infusion room or oncology wing, I appeared to be the healthiest person there. Once, I was even mistaken for a drug rep. Heck, some of the older women viewed me as eye candy.

Immediately following the first round of Panitumumab, a rash appeared at the top of my forehead and grew down the center of my face to my chin. It was so bad it looked more like severe road rash from a bike wreck than a drug's side effect.

My nose swelled, and the discomfort was almost unbearable. I felt like Job. After being diagnosed with cancer, enduring years of chemotherapy, and having a heart attack, I wondered, *What's next? Boils?* (While I have not had boils, I cannot imagine them being worse than what I experienced with that gross rash.)

That was the first time in my treatment when I looked sick. It was hard for people to look at me. Heck, it was hard for me to look at me. People would see my rash and then look away. But they didn't see me. I'm an extrovert, so this shunning made me feel lonely—judged and ostracized. I wanted to scream, like the Elephant Man, "I am NOT an animal!"

That was the first time in my treatment when I looked sick. It was hard for people to look at me. Heck, it was hard for me to look at me.

A week following the outbreak of the rash, I was scheduled to speak at the New Canaan Society in Franklin, Tennessee. A dear friend stopped by the day before to help me with my talk. As he was leaving, he said, "Greg, you oughta wear a ball cap tomorrow morning. At least the bill will cover some of that growth." As Solomon said in Proverbs 27:6, "Wounds from a friend can be trusted."

A disfiguring rash was certainly not in my plans. However, it reveals yet another paradox I've discovered on this journey: It's not about my plans. It's about being available and embracing interruptions, engaging with people at God's prompting, and trusting him for the results. This personal engagement with others has been the adventure of a lifetime and, without suffering, I would have missed it. In his mercy, God wanted me to experience life on his terms, not mine. At last, I'm discovering his terms are far better. He is teaching me to live John 10:10: "The thief comes only to steal and kill and destroy; I have come that they may have life, and have it to the full."

These days, I not only see sick people; I search for them. I now long for out-of-the-blue interruptions. Often, they are the highlights of my days. Because of the blessing of cancer, my focus has switched from my personal goals, plans, and desires to the well-being of others. Being the hands and feet of Jesus is where I've found abundant life. I've traded complexity and stress for simplicity and solace. It's the barter of a lifetime.

I've traded complexity and stress for simplicity and solace. It's the barter of a lifetime.

June 25, 2014
The Instant Camaraderie of Cancer

Last Thursday, after I completed the infusion portion of chemotherapy, I was dragging myself out of the oncology wing when I saw a young Hispanic couple sitting next to each other.

Sabina is bald, in her 30s, and battling breast cancer. Manuel, her husband, was sitting next to her, and they were engaged in conversation. As I watched, I was struck by how peaceful, happy, and in love they seemed to be.

I knew I was supposed to engage in conversation with them, so I stopped and introduced myself. Sabina and Manuel didn't have to invite me into their conversation, but they did, and they were welcoming, engaging. They were vulnerable, sharing Sabina's condition as I shared mine.

When you're in the oncology wing, there's instant camaraderie I've experienced nowhere else. There's also a deep sense of knowing and understanding because we share a similar struggle, a similar foe, a similar experience. Unless you've been there, there's no way of truly understanding. But it's remarkable. Cancer is the great equalizer.

At the end of our conversation, God told me to pray for Sabina and Manuel. Out of respect, I asked if it was ok, and they agreed. Afterward, Manuel said, "It's cool you would pray for us like that. Thank you." He then shared his father had been asking them to go to church for years. On Father's Day, he and Sabina finally agreed to go. During the altar call, Sabina let go of Manuel's hand, walked to the front of the church, and gave her life to Jesus.

Amazing. This young Hispanic man and woman are my brother and sister in Christ. We share the same faith and the same eternal destiny. What's also amazing is if I had seen Manuel anywhere else, other than the oncology wing, I would have judged him. I probably would have been afraid of him and, frankly, I would have avoided him due to the tattoos on his arms, chest, and the top of his skull. Manuel shared he was embarrassed by the tattoos. He had gotten them years earlier when he was in prison. Manuel shared that he used to be a bad guy, but for over five years he has been working hard. He loves his wife and has built a life after prison.

If I didn't have cancer, I would have never met Sabina and Manuel. My life wouldn't have been blessed by their story, their faith, and their love for each another.

Whatever you have, wherever you have been, whatever choices you have made, don't despair and don't be ashamed. See, that is where God demonstrates the full force of the gospel. That is where our depravity, our brokenness, and God's ultimate forgiveness collide.

Genesis 50:20 tells us, *"You intended to harm me, but God intended it for good to accomplish what is now being done, the saving of many lives."*

You see, God is in the redeeming business. He continues to redeem my cancer, my ultimate selfishness, my sin, Manuel's prison sentence, your divorce, your whatever.

> The incredible news is, I've been redeemed
> and forgiven–and so have you.

So, what does this have to do with you?

1. *When was the last time you allowed something or someone to interrupt your plans for the day?*

2. *What do you do when you see someone struggling with a medical condition?*

3. *How do you think it feels to be shunned because of a physical abnormality?*

EVERYONE IS BROKEN

WHEN WE ADMIT THAT WE'RE
FRACTURED, IN ONE WAY OR
ANOTHER, OTHERS WILL RISK
VULNERABILITY TOO.

"I'M DEPRESSED." Who knew those two words in a blog post would generate more than 500 responses? Harvard MBAs, corporate executives, stay-at-home moms, students, and pastors posted comments on my Facebook page.

My friend DeAnn, who has been wrestling with chronic fatigue for decades, responded, "Greg, when you share your struggles, I feel less alone in mine."

Another friend, whose young husband died of cancer early in their marriage, wrote, "Greg, thanks for sharing that. It's helpful to know someone else is being real about the difficulties of life.

A church elder, father, husband, and corporate executive told me in a private message, "I don't often struggle with depression, but I frequently struggle with anxiety. The older I get, the weaker I feel."

Struggles. We all have them. But far too often, we choose to put up facades. (I know because I lived that way for 46 years.) We hide tough times in our marriages. We camouflage drug problems or issues with alcohol. We cloak anger, grief, and financial difficulties. We don't want to talk about stuff like that because stuff like that makes us feel broken and that there's something distinctively wrong with us. So, we hole up behind the facades of our perfectly painted front doors—and we spend a lot of time and energy trying to make others believe we have it all together.

The truth? No one has it all together, and when we pretend we do, anxiety increases and life becomes even more challenging. After wrestling with cancer for five years, I've discovered everyone is broken. Everyone is struggling with something. Far too often, we are clueless about what's going on behind our neighbors' perfectly painted front doors. We have this mental image of "Ozzie and Harriet" happiness, but real life is more like the television drama "This is Us." Life is messy. Complicated. Confusing. Hard. Our neighbors struggle with all sorts of things—suicide attempts, bankruptcy, illness, battles with relatives, babies lost before birth, addictions. The challenges go on and on.

For a bit of context, I wrote that depression blog because nausea associated with chemo wasn't easing up. My energy level was rock bottom. Of course, it didn't help that it had been raining in Middle Tennessee for well over a week. I was in a downward spiral. I didn't feel inspired to write anything uplifting. On that rainy January day, I truly was depressed.

I wrote that Facebook post twice, erasing the first draft because I didn't want to sound like a whiner. Later, the same thought about depression hit me again, so I rewrote the post and just put it out there.

And you know what? Getting those 500 responses opened my eyes and made me feel less alone. See, when we admit that we're fractured, in one way or another, others will risk being vulnerable too. But someone must break the ice. Someone must be vulnerable first. Someone must admit, "I'm struggling."

THE UNEXPECTED ICEBREAKER

I've discovered, as author Ann Voskamp has, "The shortest distance between two hearts is always the way of brokenness."[9] In my brokenness, I've connected with people at the deepest levels—people of different races, genders, economic levels, and nationalities. There's not a better way to live.

> "The shortest distance between two hearts is always the way of brokenness." Ann Voskamp

In 2015, Tracey, Jackson, and I traveled to Beaver Creek, Colorado for a long weekend. While Jackson and Tracey skied, I stayed behind and relaxed in the lobby of the Park Hyatt Resort. Floor-to-ceiling windows, through which you can take in the energy and beauty of the magestic mountain, showcase the back wall of the spacious, vaulted room.

On a sunny but icy-cold day, I sat in my favorite leather chair by the wood-burning fireplace, enjoying a long morning of writing in my journal, reading my Bible, and catching up on email. Later, I headed across the room in a quest for the best Cabernet I could find. While making my selection, I engaged in small talk with the bartender, a 30-something woman named Alicia.

She asked, "Why aren't you skiing today?"

"Do you really want to know?"

"Well, of course. I asked, didn't I?"

"Yes, you did. Well, I have Stage IV colon cancer, which has moved to my lungs. This week I endured my 48th round of chemo. The treatment started on Monday and concluded on Wednesday, so today I'm nauseated and weak. I love being in the mountains, but at this altitude, breathing is difficult for me, and skiing is impossible. Interesting though, while some may call having cancer a curse, I can honestly say I have never felt more alive."

"Why?" Alicia asked.

"Well, here's my theory: I love my 13-year-old son deeply; however, I believe God loves you and me even more, if that's possible. So, because he loves me, he doesn't intend cancer as a curse or to harm me. God intends it as something good."

"Would you be ok if I came over to discuss this with you in greater detail?" Alicia asked. "I need to serve this table, and then I will be right over."

"Of course, I'm in the leather chair by the fireplace."

After several minutes, Alicia made her way across the room. She leaned against the sofa across from my chair and said, "My father was a Baptist pastor in Florida. He died seven years ago of a massive heart attack, completely unexpected. Since then, I've turned my back on God and moved in the opposite direction. You wouldn't believe what I have done with my life. About a year ago, I decided I would end it all. So, I planned to kill myself on a Saturday. Just minutes before I went through with it, a Baptist pastor knocked on my apartment door and invited my sister and me to his church. He doesn't know this, but he saved my life."

"God loves you. It doesn't matter what you've done or where you've been. God is crazy in love with you. Really, you are forgiven."

Alicia averted her eyes as she shared her story. She appeared ashamed of who she had become since her father's passing.

Deep inside, I felt God telling me to stand and speak softly in Alicia's ear. So, I stood, approached her slowly, and said what I was prompted to say:

"God loves you. It doesn't matter what you've done or where you've been. God is crazy in love with you. Really, you are forgiven."

As soon as I finished those four sentences, Alicia began sobbing and grabbed me in the biggest bear hug you can imagine. All the while, I continued to tell her, "God loves you deeply. You are forgiven." I knew what I was saying to Alicia came directly from God, but I also sensed I was serving as a surrogate father for that young woman.

Now, how in the world did a personal exchange of that intensity and depth happen between two strangers? Think about it. At the time, I was a chubby 50-year-old man with the cool factor of zero. However, within a matter of minutes, I had connected at the heart level with a young bartender with whom I had almost nothing in common—except we were both broken, in need of forgiveness, and desperate for our Heavenly Father's love and acceptance.

Before my cancer diagnosis, stuff like this never happened. Frankly, I was too busy—always on some mission. Sure, I'm a people person; I can easily converse with anyone. But broken people like Alicia weren't on my radar screen. I was moving way too fast to connect deeply with strangers. God used cancer to slow me down—and that's a good thing. Now, below-the-surface interactions are more common than not. For me, the joy of genuinely connecting with another human being is second to none. Whenever it happens, it's the best part of my day. And for me, it would have never happened without slowing down, vulnerability, and a shared brokenness.

Before cancer forced me to hit the pause button, I seldom considered leading a conversation with anything other than the perfect image I felt compelled to portray. Brokenness has taught me when I'm vulnerable and honestly communicate what's going on in my life health-wise—and where I see God in it—my new friends get permission to reciprocate.

A few months after I met Alicia, I was back in Beaver Creek with Tracey and Jackson for another long weekend. When we entered the Park Hyatt lounge area, Alicia immediately stopped what she was doing and ran to meet us. Her greeting for me was a big hug and a kiss on the cheek, followed by the best compliment I've ever received in the form of a question. Alicia asked, "How is my favorite human?" Alicia blessed me with that title because God used my weakness to connect with hers—and I listened to what his voice was telling me to do in that encounter.

Through both planned appointments and unexpected encounters with strangers, I've grown to love the individuals God has graciously placed in my path. He is teaching me a lot about the power of vulnerability.

These encounters are life-giving blessings, and I'm incredibly thankful for them.

> When we listen to what God wants to do through us, we connect with others. Relationships deepen. Hope grows. And we feel less alone.

Bottom line? We're all broken. If we're willing to admit brokenness, we don't have to shoulder burdens alone. When we listen to what God wants to do through us, we connect with others. Relationships deepen. Hope grows. And we feel less alone.

Yes, Ann, "the shortest distance between two hearts is always the way of brokenness."[10]

> *But he said to me, 'My grace is sufficient for you, for my power is made perfect in weakness.' Therefore, I will boast all the more gladly about my weaknesses, so that Christ's power may rest on me. That is why, for Christ's sake, I delight in weaknesses, in insults, in hardships, in persecutions, in difficulties. For when I am weak, then I am strong. 2 Corinthians 12:9-10*

July 19, 2014
Elliott's Hardware: A Holy Place

This afternoon, as I was driving to Elliott's Hardware, I was sad and depressed. Honestly, I wanted to pull over to the side of the road and cry. It felt as though everything had built up in me emotionally, and the dam was about to break.

What had built up?

- The results of my last CT scan.
- The clutter we are living in as we unpack boxes in our newly renovated home is overwhelming to me.
- The never-ending list of things that must be addressed in our home to make it right.
- Jackson. How do I encourage him to get out of the house, build friendships in our neighborhood, become active, and not just stare at a computer screen playing Xbox Minecraft®?

I was headed to Elliott's to purchase bolts for our washing machine and fertilizer for our yard. However, God had something else in mind.

As I entered the hardware store, God intercepted me and placed Gary and Hope in my path.

Gary is probably 50 years old. He was walking with the help of two hiking poles, and he was wearing a golf hat and a surgical mask. Hope was walking to his left, holding his elbow.

Immediately I was prompted to stop and engage in conversation with them. "Cancer? I asked." In a raspy air-filled voice Gary's response was, "No, I have antitrypsin deficiency (COPD). In March, I had a double lung transplant."

Gary looked at Hope, his beautiful 24-year-old daughter, and said, "Hope had cancer when she was eight, and it returned when she was ten. In both cases, she had to undergo four days of radiation back to back to prepare for bone marrow transplants. She has a birthday next week. She will be 25, and she is cancer-free."

We discussed my cancer, and then I was prompted to ask, in the middle of Elliott's Hardware, if I could pray for them. "Of course," Gary said, "but only if we can pray for you too."

So today, at 1:00 pm, Elliot's Hardware became a holy place—a chapel, if you will, as Gary, Hope, and I grasped hands, bowed our heads, and prayed for one another. It was beautiful, and outside of Gary's weakened state, my battle, and Hope's victory, it would have never happened.

Following this experience, I realized when I start to get depressed and sad, it is, for the most part, because I'm thinking about myself. However, when I look outward, when I respond to God's prompting to pray for or serve others, when I say *yes* to the prompting to be the hands and feet of Jesus, then I am blessed.

Thank you, God. Thank you, Gary. Thank you, Hope. You made my day.

Gary is sick. I am too. However, Hope is a miracle, a miracle who loves Jesus. And that is strikingly beautiful.

January 13, 2016
Are You Wearing a Mask?

The reason we never really get to know those around us is that we've been trained to keep our smiley-happy masks on. Today, I had lunch with a friend, and we did just the opposite. As we ate and talked, we shared our hurts and concerns. We talked about where we are. We were vulnerable. We shared things we had done and regretted, and we found solace in one another. There was a bit of eye water too. It was refreshing.

Our young server, Holly, had a fresh new tattoo on her right arm that reads, "God, grant me the serenity to accept the things I cannot change, the courage to change the things I can, and the wisdom to know the difference."

My friend asked her about it, and she replied, "Yes, this tattoo is a constant reminder to me. See, I'm in recovery."

Wow! This young lady gets it! She was vulnerable. She ripped off her mask right in front of us and in so doing she encouraged my friend and me to do the same.

Immediately I said, "Holly, thank you for being vulnerable. We're all broken. We're all dealing with something. I have Stage IV cancer; my friend has his stuff, and that's ok. Everyone in this restaurant has something they're dealing with; however, most of them are good at hiding it."

After a brief conversation, I asked Holly if it would be ok if we prayed for her. She mentioned when we were blessing our meal she was compelled to join us, but couldn't get to our table in time. So, right there in a crowded restaurant, we stopped and prayed for our new friend. That table with four chairs and three broken people became a holy place; it became church for a few minutes this afternoon.

What are you dealing with? What load are you carrying alone? Are you suffering in silence?

It doesn't have to be that way.

There is freedom in vulnerability. There is liberty in understanding we're all broken, and it's healthy to share the load with others. Take off your mask and embrace authentic relationship with those you may call friends who don't know the real you.

Is there risk in living this way? Yes, but the reward is far greater.

So, what does this have to do with you?

1. How are you broken?

2. What mask do you wear most often?

3. When was the last time you admitted to someone that you struggle?

GOD'S MATH

DOING GOD'S WILL GOD'S WAY PROVIDES A MULTIPLICATION EFFECT I NEVER EXPERIENCED WHEN I FOCUSED ON MY SIMPLE ADDITION PLAN.

I'VE BEEN TO THE EDGE, AND THE ANSWER IS NO. Because of an out-of-the-blue heart attack that sucked the air out of my lungs, I no longer wonder if I'll be afraid when I breathe my last breath on earth. It's good to know this. Seriously. It gave me the gift of perspective. So, I'm not scared to take my last breath. I'm focused on making the ones I breathe before that last one count.

During the weeks before my first heart attack, (yes, there was round two), I had coughed a lot and assumed it was the cancer in my lungs. There were also numerous occasions when I would attempt to walk a mile in our neighborhood, only to be forced to stop—gasping, hands on knees, on the verge of throwing up. Now I know a clogged artery, not cancer, was the culprit.

> I'm not scared to take my last breath. I'm focused on making the ones I breathe before that last one count.

As I write this, it almost feels as though I'm referring to someone else. See, five years ago, I was the guy who ran every day, lifted weights, biked, and ate right. I took care of myself. But here I am, just a few days past my 52nd birthday, wrestling with cancer and a weak heart.

The first chest pain hit me in the wee morning hours of April 7, 2016. God bless my sweet wife.

I had to jolt Tracey out of bed to drive me to the emergency room. Once there, things got bad. I was coughing up blood and barely able to suck in shallow breaths. The docs considered putting me on a ventilator. Tracey prayed against this because my mom died of complications from colon cancer, and the beginning of the end for her was the ventilator.

While lying there, gasping for air, three things came to mind.

First, I was thankful Tracey and Jackson know Jesus. There was no doubt in my mind that if my life were to end, I would see them again.

Second, I was thankful members of our church (think small group) were in the waiting room with Tracey and Jackson, taking care of them. If I didn't make it, I knew that tender care would continue.

Third, I looked around the room and wondered, *Does that nurse know Jesus? How about that doctor?*

Never once during those brutal 37 hours in the ICU did I think, *I wish we had bought the bigger, faster Lexus LS instead of the ES.* Nor did I think, *I wish we had built a bigger home.* I also didn't lament, *Gosh, I wish I had done that business deal. It would have made a lot of money.* No, during that time when oxygen was sparse it became crystal clear to me what matters.

When everything is said and done, the words of God and the souls of men are the only things that last. If I invest my greatest commodity—time—in anything else, I'm wasting it.

When everything is said and done, the words of God and the souls of men are the only things that last.

Throughout that April morning and early afternoon, I rested on and off until the doctors finally determined they needed to insert a stent in my heart. They informed us the heart attack had left me with 60 percent capacity—and only time would tell if that would improve.

THE MIRACLE OF MULTIPLICATION

On Friday afternoon, I asked Tracey for my laptop because I had a blog thought I wanted to capture. Country music legend Hank Williams once said, "People don't write music. It's given to them."[11] I couldn't agree more. It's not uncommon for me to feel prompted to write something and then minutes later look at my computer screen and wonder where what I had just written came from. I often write such posts through tears. The post I wrote the day after my heart attack was one of those. It's titled "I Can Breathe . . . Barely." (I've included it at the end of this chapter.) In the post, I recounted how the previous 37 hours hadn't gone as planned. The heart attack had interrupted not only my life but the lives of others as well.

I posted the blog and tried to get some rest.

On Sunday morning, April 10, Tracey and I were in my hospital room when, almost simultaneously, our phones started blowing up. For a few minutes, the dings and chimes of numerous texts and emails sounded like a pinball machine in high gear.

We soon discovered our friend and former pastor, Todd Wagner, at Watermark Community Church in Dallas had used my Facebook post as a sermon illustration during four church services that morning. At Watermark, my blog post was viewed and heard by approximately 18,000 people.

Later, we discovered a pastor in Houston, one in Little Rock, and another in Lexington also had used the same post as a sermon illustration.

Back when I was working full time, I would strategically develop a plan and then operate against the plan, ruthlessly avoiding interruptions. As I've previously stated, there's nothing wrong with having a plan. A plan can get you places. However, I was working my plan motivated by a sense of performing for my Heavenly Father. I rarely asked for his opinion, much less direction.

It recently dawned on me that I don't recall being interrupted much when I was employed full time. My working plan produced good results: 1 + 1 = 2. Things seemed to add up well. It was growth.

But this side of cancer and two heart attacks, I now realize all that Murtha-induced growth was growth by simple addition. It was Murtha math, not God's. God's math is multiplication.

It was Murtha math, not God's. God's math is multiplication.

Now, let's reflect on what happened with the "I Can Breathe . . . Barely" post. God prompted me with a thought. In obedience, I merely typed out where I was, what I was experiencing, including the story of Angel, my nurse, whom God sent my way.

Less than 45 hours later, approximately 20,000 people in three states were influenced by my thoughts. Doing God's will God's way provides a multiplication effect I never experienced when I focused on my addition plan.

Recently, I had a conversation with my brother about the feasibility of being a successful business-person fully in tune to the prompting of the Holy Spirit. I asked, "Zac, is it possible to be a business success while being in tune with what God is leading you to do?"

His response? "Yes, I think it's possible; however, I believe your definition of success would probably migrate."

As I ponder this thought, I think of my friend Bob Muzikowski, founder of Chicago Hope Academy and author of the inspiring book *Safe at Home*, who once told me, "Greg, when we consider the Bible story of the Good Samaritan, we must remember that act of kindness took time. It was an out-of-the-blue interruption in this man's day. The Good Samaritan took the time to take to a hotel a bloody, beaten-up stranger he found on the side of the road. Once there, he negotiated a rate and paid the innkeeper to provide lodging and care for the needs of that man."

Bob went on to say, "You know what? The Samaritan's action took time, cost him money, and he was probably late to his next appointment. Who knows? Maybe he even lost business that day."

The scenario begs this question: Should professional success be our goal? American Catholic writer and theologian Thomas Merton had a stout opinion of success:

> *If I had a message to my contemporaries it is surely this: Be anything you like, be madmen, drunks, and bastards of every shape and form, but at all costs avoid one thing: success . . . If you are too obsessed with success, you will forget to live. If you have learned only how to be a success, your life has probably been wasted.*[12]

As I've traveled Cancer Road, I've been forced to slow down. My life has dramatically changed. My values have changed. Our family lives on a lot less money. But my life has never been richer.

Gone are the days when I'm focused on my personal goals and meeting the next quarter's earnings. My impact is far more significant now that I realize this is not my story, it's God's. See, God has a plan, and if we play the role he has for us versus creating one for ourselves, then we've got it made. I've discovered life is less taxing and far more productive when I live in obedience to what God leads me to do and not the other way around. Trust, me. God's math works.

> Life is less taxing and far more productive when I live in obedience to what God leads me to do and not the other way around. Trust, me. God's math works.

I haven't yet taken my last breath. I'm still here. Hopefully, you'll join me in making every breath count.

April 8, 2016
I Can Breathe . . . Barely

It has been an out-of-the-blue 37 hours.

Thursday at 2:30 a.m., I woke with severe chest pains. *Where is this pain coming from?* I wondered, *Did I bruise my lungs from all the coughing?*

Taking no chances, Tracey and I rushed to Williamson Medical Center, where they admitted me for cardiac arrest. Yes, although they located two blood clots in my lungs, I was experiencing a heart attack in real time.

Thank God, we were in the hospital when this was going on. There were people with knowledge leading us through the process of what we should do, which was life-saving.

Since then, I have had a stent placed in the front part of my heart. The docs say I lost 40 percent of this part of my heart's functioning capacity, but I could see a reversal in this if we're fortunate. I pray we are fortunate.

We're now facing an intricately complicated health puzzle. Having a stent requires the use of blood thinners, which in turn can cause significant bleeding in my cancer-filled lungs. The dance will be to determine how much blood thinner we can use while avoiding bleeding.

Yesterday morning our nurse was a tiny 30-something young woman named Angel. Angel was born two months premature and weighed in at a whopping 1.5 lbs. After her birth, she lost down to .5 pounds and wasn't expected to make it. Her parents, afraid to name her, asked the nurses to help, and she was called their "little angel."

Tracey and I held Angel's hands and challenged her by asking, "Angel, why would God allow you to emerge from a beginning like that without having big plans for you? We believe God has big plans for you." We prayed with Angel that she would see what the plans were and embrace them.

I'm still here. I've recently endured a major heart attack, 50 rounds of chemotherapy, and I find it almost impossible to breathe. But while there is breath in my lungs, I will use it to praise Jesus. I will use it to encourage Angel and people like her. I will continue this out-of-the-blue adventure of a lifetime.

Will you join me? If you do, you'll never regret it.

November 23, 2014
I'm Afraid

Thursday, while I was at Texas Oncology at Baylor, a sweet 74-year-old lady sat next to me enduring her 20th round of chemo.

Nora is beautiful and still has her hair. She is a mother and grandmother. Nora is tiny, weighing in at 94 pounds. She has a lot of spunk and is amazingly inquisitive.

When she sat beside me, Nora said, "My, aren't you handsome!"

(You may not realize this, but I'm eye candy in infusion rooms for the over-70 crowd.)

Nora: What are you here for?

Me: Colon cancer.

Nora: Me too. What stage?

Me: Stage IV

Nora: Me too. Who is your doctor?

Me: Dr. McCollum.

Nora: Me too.

Nora: I'm afraid. Are you?

That was where our similarities stopped.

Me: No, I have never been afraid of cancer.

Nora: Why not?

Me: Do you have kids, Nora?

Nora: Yes.

Me: Do you love them?

Nora: Absolutely.

Me: I have a 12-year-old son, and I love him with everything in me. Frankly, I believe our Heavenly Father loves us even more than we love our children. Do you want what's best for your children?

Nora: Yes, I do.

Me: I believe our Heavenly Father wants what's best for you and me and since this is the case, then having cancer must be a part of his plan. He is God, and I trust Him. Since I was 19, I've been reading the Bible and trying to follow Jesus.

Nora: So, you feel good about the chips you've earned?

Me: Chips? No. There is nothing I could do to earn God's grace. Grace is a gift to anyone who will take it.

Me: Would you allow me to pray for you?

Nora: Are you a pastor?

Me: No. I'm just a business guy who is a lot like you.

Nora: Yes, I would like that.

We prayed. I held Nora's hand. I asked God to heal her and give her peace, to eliminate her fear.

Nora: Greg, when you prayed I felt warm inside.

Friends, I have no clue why Nora felt warm inside. What I am blown away by is that I didn't approach her. She sat next to me and initiated our conversation. She asked all the questions and then vulnerably shared she was afraid. I simply followed God's lead.

If you are afraid, do not be. Those who place their faith in Jesus are promised an eternity with him—an eternity promised to be much better than our present reality. Where we are going is better than where we are. What God has given me and what I have experienced on this earth have been terrific, and to think heaven will be even better is amazing.

Please, place your faith in Jesus and embrace the future with me—with no fear.

So, what does this have to do with you?

1. *If you landed in the ICU and were unable to breathe, would you be afraid?*

2. *What is your definition of success and where do you invest most of your time given that perspective?*

3. *How would a close brush with death change your priorities?*

GUMBALL THEOLOGY

WHAT'S THE GOAL OF OUR EXISTENCE ON THIS PLANET? IS IT TO SAIL UNSCATHED TO THE GRAVE FOR 70-PLUS YEARS WITH NO REAL CHALLENGES? NO. OUR GOAL ON EARTH SHOULDN'T BE LONGEVITY BUT OBEDIENCE, AS THIS LEADS TO PURPOSE AND ADVENTURE!

I'M A BETTER MAN WHEN I'M SICK. As my body has grown weaker, my faith has never been stronger. For years, I raced ahead of God, working my life plan in hyper mode. I was a complicated, highly driven mess. Cancer has taught me to simplify my faith by listening to God and simply doing what he asks me to do. I no longer live in high-anxiety performance mode but the open posture of obedience.

That's why I'm a better man when I'm sick. God used my illness to slow me down so I would join his plan instead of pushing my agenda forward my way. If I had to choose between the lessons of cancer and a healthy life on my own, I would choose cancer.

> If I had to choose between the lessons of cancer and a healthy life on my own, I would choose cancer.

While others may view my cancer as a curse, I see it as a fresh opportunity to get life right. Because what's the goal of our existence on this planet? Is it to sail unscathed to the grave for 70-plus years with no real challenges? *No.* Our goal on earth shouldn't be longevity but obedience, as this leads to purpose and adventure!

Obedience is far more natural when I'm forced to rely on God. When I started practicing this behavior, it was a bit uncomfortable; however, after a while, it has become easier to consistently say *yes* to Jesus—and the still small voice that leads me to his bigger story.

Recently I had a conversation with my friend Joe Millspaugh. Joe's dad, Clark, was one of the best men I've ever known. Joe found out he had leukemia in January of 2012, one day before I received my diagnosis.

Clark knew he was in a battle for his life, but with complete clarity and conviction he told Joe, "Son, I plan on fighting this disease, and I pray I'll live, but either way, I'm golden."

Joe told me he asked his dad, "Are you afraid?"

Clark responded with a brief flare of anger.

"Yes, I am—when I focus on my own small-ass story. But I choose to focus on God and his plan for my life. When I do, the fear seems to go away. For ten years, I've been following Jesus, and I've encouraged others to do the same. Now, when my faith is being tested, is the time to cling to Jesus, and I intend to do just that."

Clark had hundreds, if not thousands, of people praying for his healing. We prayed God would eradicate Clark's cancer and give him back his life. Trust me, if ever a person deserved healing, it was Clark Millspaugh. But approximately ten months after his diagnosis, my friend went to be with Jesus.

One of my pet peeves is when I read a Facebook post or hear someone say, "God is so good! I prayed the test results would return negative, and he answered my prayers. *God. Is. So. Good.*" (Frankly, this statement makes me angry, so I guess it's a bit more than a pet peeve.)

I like to call such declarations Gumball Theology. If I grab a quarter and place it in a gumball machine, then I'm certain to receive a gumball. The only real question is what color or flavor it will be?

The goodness of God has nothing to do with whether he answers our prayers in the way we want them answered. God created the universe. He knew each of us before we were in the womb. God sacrificed his one and only Son to reestablish a relationship with us after Adam and Eve allowed sin to enter Eden.

God is good because he is God. Period.

> The goodness of God has nothing to do with whether he answers our prayers in the way we want them answered. God is good because he is God. Period.

WAS THAT A MIRACLE?

A close friend recently told me that during a time of family prayer, his youngest son said, "Dad, Mr. Murtha must have really deep faith because we

84

have been praying for his healing for years and he hasn't been healed, but he still loves Jesus."

Yes, I've prayed for healing for five years. Hundreds of people around the globe pray for my healing too. Why not me? Why has God not chosen to heal me? I would welcome the opportunity to boast of God's goodness in this way. Do I not have the right amount of faith? Do I not trust him like I say I do? Or maybe, it is simply a part of God's larger plan for me?

> Why has God not chosen to heal me? Do I not have the right amount of faith? Do I not trust him like I say I do? Or maybe, it is simply a part of God's larger plan for me?

Remember the Daniel 3 story, when Shadrach, Meshach, and Abednego refused to bow to a foreign god? Even with the threat of being thrown into a furnace, these three men said, "King Nebuchadnezzar, we do not need to defend ourselves before you in this matter. If we are thrown into the blazing furnace, the God we serve is able to deliver us from it, and he will deliver us from Your Majesty's hand. But even if he does not, we want you to know, Your Majesty, that we will not serve your gods or worship the image of gold you have set up."

That "even if" place is where I've landed on my journey through illness with potentially no noticeable miracle of healing. The lyrics to the MercyMe song "Even If," co-written by Bart Millard and Tim Timmons, express exactly how I feel. (Add this incredibly honest song from the *Lifer* album to your playlist today.) I listen to it often because the lyrics resound in my soul. Like Bart Millard, I know God can heal me from cancer because he is Almighty God. But *even if* physical healing is not his plan for me, I trust him. My hope rests in him alone. It's a comforting place to rest my future.

Besides, I may have experienced miracles after all.

I've endured 75 rounds of chemotherapy—with no sign of letting up. Every time I receive another treatment, doctors order labs, and every time my blood work has been stellar. My doctors are amazed. Maybe this is an answered prayer—or maybe even a miracle?

Following my first heart attack, I couldn't walk ten feet without the use of oxygen. That attack hit six weeks before a scheduled trip to Central Europe. Two friends and I planned to travel to Krakow, Poland, to experience Auschwitz. Next, we were to head to Berlin to tour the home of Dietrich Bonhoeffer, my favorite theologian, and to see the 1936 Olympics stadium. My doctor laughed when I said, "Doc, you have six weeks to make me better. I have an eleven-day trip scheduled to Central Europe, and I want to take it."

He responded summarily, "That's not going to happen."

I didn't cancel the trip. Instead, I prayed, along with my co-travelers, Gary Jones and Ted Dickey.

One week after being released from the hospital, Tracey and I went to my cardiologist's office for a checkup. As I walked by the doctor's station, I noticed he stopped what he was doing and watched me.

A few minutes later, he joined Tracey and me in the examination room. He didn't say a word. He just walked over, listened to my heart, backed away, and said, "Greg, I have no way of explaining your recovery, outside of a miracle." He went on to say, "I'm not giving you permission to take your trip to Central Europe; I'm ordering you to go. It will be good for you."

Was it a miracle I got to experience that incredible trip to Central Europe? Was it a miracle that one year after that heart attack, I was in Aspen, Colorado, writing this book? Is it a miracle I have hope for a future I intend to embrace with boldness and joy?

I don't know if these are miracles, but I do know God is good, whether he answers my prayers in the way I ask or not.

And I also know it is well with my soul.

April 28, 2016
Magic Happens Through Weakness

This morning at the New Canaan Society, Nate Larkin spoke. He was incredibly vulnerable and well spoken. He confessed that he, too, wrestled with why God hadn't healed him. Then he said, "The Apostle Paul begged to have his thorn removed too."

> *Three times I pleaded with the Lord to take it away from me. But he said to me, 'My grace is sufficient for you, for my power is made perfect in weakness.' Therefore I will boast all the more gladly about my weaknesses, so that Christ's power may rest on me.*
> *2 Corinthians 12:8-9*

Nate said he believes God loves him too much to take away his thorn. He believes it is the only lever large enough to keep him dependent on God. He confessed he needs that dependency more than the healing he has requested.

Frankly, I have discovered life is far richer with my struggle than it was without it. It leads me to places where there are people who need to hear what I have to say. It forces me to slow down every other week and make eye contact with God during chemo infusions. It makes me solely dependent upon him, and there's not a better place to be.

As the Apostle Paul shared, *"My grace is sufficient for you, for my power is made perfect in weakness . . . for when I am weak, then I am strong."*

I've discovered the magic happens through weakness, through suffering, through tears, and when I am forced to cry out. The true connection comes through pain, so I am inclined to ask people to stop praying for my healing. Yes, a better prayer would be for God to glorify himself in my weakness. I believe this is closer to God's heart if we're honest with one another. And the power of prayer is when it changes our hearts to be closer to God's, not the other way around.

See, he's God; he knows better. This adventure is his story, not mine. Yes, his power is made perfect in my weakness—and that's a good thing.

May 30, 2014
Jackson Humor: I'm Awesome!

I'm a better man when I'm sick, but a good laugh is great medicine. This afternoon, while driving through Brentwood, Tennessee, I was discussing the issue of entitlement with Tracey. Frankly, I didn't even know Jackson was listening to our conversation until I heard him ask, "Dad, what does entitlement mean?"

I replied, "Well, son, it reminds me of you. Entitlement is when you expect people to give you things just because you are you."

Jackson's prompt response was, "Dad, that's not me at all. I don't expect people to give me stuff because I'm me. I expect them to give me stuff because I'm AWESOME."

Entitlement may be an issue in our family, but a sense of self-worth obviously is not.

f

So, what does this have to do with you?

1. *Would you say yes to a chronic illness if you knew it would lead you to a deep relationship with the Creator of the Universe?*

2. *What does it mean to say, "I'm a better man when I'm sick"?*

3. *Do you tend to focus on your plan or God's larger plan for your life?*

WHAT'S IN YOUR BUCKET?

TOO MUCH SELFLESSNESS IS
NOT HEALTHY FOR ANYONE
ON ANY LEVEL. IF WE DON'T
KEEP OUR BUCKETS FILLED,
SERVING OTHERS IS
UNSUSTAINABLE.

TRACEY'S BUCKET WAS EMPTY. The early days of my cancer treatment were brutal. All eyes were on me, including my own. The world revolved around me and how I was feeling. But when someone is battling a chronic illness, a caregiver can get drained. Quickly.

The last drops drained out of Tracey's bucket on a cold, dark, rainy Valentine's Day in 2015. For most of our friends, that day meant dinner at a romantic restaurant. For Tracey and me, it was chemo week. I hadn't eaten for three days. We didn't have the anti-nausea drugs dialed in, and the treatments were a real beating. I threw up 17 times in less than 60 hours, and nothing was working to alleviate the sickness. Later, I learned Tracey would go outside and pull weeds in our flower gardens to avoid hearing the retching. While what I was experiencing was physically wrenching, it was excruciatingly hard on Tracey too.

As my caregiver, Tracey is always attempting to make sure I'm eating properly and encouraging me to hydrate. Valentine's Saturday, things were no different.

The last drops drained out of Tracey's bucket on a cold, dark, rainy Valentine's Day in 2015.

She knew I didn't have an appetite, but she recognized I needed to eat something—anything—so she asked if I would like for her to go to our favorite Thai restaurant to get my first-choice meal, Red Curry Chicken. Deep inside, I knew I probably wouldn't eat much, but I decided to give it a shot. The restaurant was less than a mile from our Dallas home, so it was convenient for us to pick up a to-go order. When Tracey departed, I expected her to return quickly. But she didn't.

Later I learned when Tracey exited the restaurant parking lot, she turned left instead of right. She missed the sign that read *No Left Turn*, and a police officer was there to remind her of the oversight.

Tracey was driving my car, and when the officer asked her for the registration and proof of insurance, she couldn't find the papers. The officer became terse and accusatory. When he took my wife's driver's license back to his car, the last drop from Tracey's bucket drained onto Forest Lane in North Dallas.

What happens when your bucket is bone dry? Everyone is different, but that dark, cold evening, Tracey started sobbing. After caring for me nonstop for weeks, she simply had nothing left. It's in these times that 1 + 1 can equal 236. This reality blindsided both of us.

When the officer returned, Tracey said between sobs, "Officer, it's a tough time for my family. My husband has cancer and hasn't eaten in three days.

It's Valentine's Day, and I'm trying to take him a meal. Everyone else is enjoying dinner at their favorite restaurant, and I am driving, by myself, to a restaurant, in the rain, hoping to do something that will help."

Instead of backing off, the officer demanded Tracey hand him her car keys. Then he called an ambulance. *I'm not kidding.*

Did Tracey break the law? *Yes.* Was she at the complete bottom of her emotional bucket? *Absolutely.* Was it the officer's fault Tracey's bucket was empty? *No.*

Thankfully, another officer intervened to keep Tracey in her car. When my wife finally returned home—with three traffic tickets I might add—she was shaken, frustrated, angry, hurt, bewildered, and emotionally spent. In this instance, 1 + 1 equaled 2,000.

It was then I realized something wasn't right. While I understood Tracey's frustration, I didn't grasp the source of the sobbing.

Soon after this experience, Tracey and I visited a counselor. After listening to our story, the counselor turned to my wife and gently asked, "What fills your bucket, Tracey?"

Candidly, I'm ashamed to say, at that time, I had no idea what filled my wife's bucket—what made her come alive. But when Tracey began listing things, I wrote them in permanent marker on my heart:

1. Lunch with friends
2. Beach and mountain trips
3. Trips with groups of like-minded people
4. Creating beauty on a budget
5. Educating parents of kids with special needs
6. Hosting guests in our home

For months, Tracey had focused on me and my illness, Jackson and his education, our move, and the renovation of our home—as well as the everyday cooking, grocery shopping, and housekeeping. It never dawned on us she needed to fill her bucket first, and then assist Jackson and me.

Please hear me—this chapter is not about failure. To the contrary, it's about Tracey being a rock star, an amazing wife, an excellent mom, and a selfless helpmate. However, too much selflessness is not healthy for anyone on any level. If we do not keep our buckets filled, serving others is unsustainable.

> Too much selflessness is not healthy for anyone on any level. If we do not keep our buckets filled, serving others is unsustainable.

WISDOM FOR CAREGIVERS

Caregivers usually take a backseat to those they nurture and rarely do caregivers have caregivers of their own. People often ask Tracey, "How are you doing?" Sometimes, she gives a measured response. With close friends and family, she has replied, "Well, that's a loaded question. Most days, life goes on as usual with the typical ups and downs. Other days, I'm depressed and can't seem to shake it. But fear rarely visits me. I can count on one hand the number of times I've felt fear as the byproduct of cancer entering our family. I know God loves me, and I'm precious to him. He wants the best for me, even more so than my mom wants the best for me. God's plan does not look like mine. His plan is better than mine—maybe not easier, but better. He will give me what I need to get through, so I can experience real joy amidst the suffering. I've always known happiness depends on circumstances, but joy does not depend on circumstances. I am currently living with joy and holding fast to Romans 8:37-39."

> "God's plan does not look like mine. His plan is better than mine—maybe not easier, but better."
> Tracey Murtha

> *No, in all these things we are more than con-*
> *querors through him who loved us. For I am*
> *convinced that neither death nor life, neither*
> *angels nor demons, neither the present nor*
> *the future, nor any powers, neither height*
> *nor depth, nor anything else in all creation,*
> *will be able to separate us from the love of*
> *God that is in Christ Jesus our Lord.*

I'm married to a wise woman who is beautiful inside and out. Now that I know what fills Tracey's bucket, I try to help her keep it filled, and she does the same. She has also embraced wisdom our counselor gave us, along with tips other caregivers have shared with her.

1. You're not superhuman. Cut yourself some slack. Jesus will provide what you cannot—or should not. Trust him with your loved one. If you can't trust the Savior of the world, then you can't trust. Trust the one who died for you.

   > *'For I know the plans I have for you,'*
   > *declares the Lord, 'plans to prosper you and*
   > *not to harm you, plans to give you hope and*
   > *a future.' Jeremiah 29:11*

2. Know what fills your bucket and when you need to do some filling. Do it without guilt. Make a list.

3. Surround yourself with prayer warriors who pray for your loved one and you as the primary caregiver. (Consider calling a convent in your area. Nuns are faithful to pray.)

4. Accept love and help in whatever form it comes. You need help, and people want to help you.

   Above all, love each other deeply, because love covers over a multitude of sins. 1 Peter 4:8

5. Ask for help when you need it. People relate to vulnerability and weakness more than strengths or successes. There are individuals with a wealth of knowledge in the areas of your need—and they want to help. Most have walked challenging roads. They experience joy by using what they've learned along the way to help someone like you. If you don't know anyone skilled in an area of need, put it out on Facebook or ask a friend to put it out there on your behalf. Share responsibility as much as you can so you are freed up to do only the things you need to be doing.

6. Don't worry that you are a burden. When the burdens get spread around to people with expertise in those areas, the load lightens—and blessings for all abound.

7. Express gratitude in some way every day. When you focus on what you're thankful for, the hard stuff pales in comparison. Thank your Heavenly Father for your troubles because, most times, beautiful things come from refinement fire. We may not see it now, but others will.

8. Cast out fear by trusting that your Heavenly Father loves you more than you can ever imagine—way more than anyone else on this earth can or ever will. God wants the best for you and will take care of you now and in the future.

"What the world needs is people who have come alive." Howard Thurman

Can anyone of you by worrying add a single hour to your life? Therefore, do not worry about tomorrow for tomorrow will worry about itself. Each day has enough trouble of its own. Matthew 6:27, 34

Do you know what fills your bucket? What makes you come alive? It's ok to know this; as a matter of fact, it's healthy. Take the time to create a list of things that fill your bucket. And then fill it regularly. When you do, everyone benefits.

Howard Thurman—author, theologian, and civil rights leader—says it best:

> *Don't ask what the world needs. Ask what makes you come alive, and go do it. Because what the world needs is people who have come alive.*[13]

Fill your bucket and come alive.

April 10, 2017
An Unsustainable Trajectory

Last week, while I was waiting for my chemo infusion, I met a couple who moved from Memphis to Nashville to be closer to Vanderbilt University Medical Center. Brian is a sales manager for a large paper company, and his wife, Suzanne, hasn't worked in two years.

Brian is a cancer survivor. Leukemia. And although he beat the disease, the bone marrow used to fight the rogue cells has begun attacking his organs. Brian's lungs are crusty around the edges, making it difficult for him to get a deep breath.

Just three years ago, Brian was a triathlete, running most every day and competing in races. His running provided an outlet for extended days and the inevitable stress that came with leading a sales team.

Candidly, as I looked at this couple, it appeared to me as if Brian could be Suzanne's father. He is thin, stooped at the shoulders, and has scaly skin around his face. He looks 20 years older than his bride, and he's not.

Suzanne said she had left a job she was thriving in. They also sold the home she loved, and are now attending a church that is ok but not what they had given up. She also lamented that in two years she had gained 30 pounds.

Tracey and I have discovered caregivers must take care of themselves or they won't be able to maintain the riggers associated with this demanding role. When I gently told Suzanne that I didn't feel what she was doing was sustainable, she agreed; however, she feels stuck. Suzanne is fully committed to her husband and believes she needs to be there with him until the end. However, whenever she considers doing something for herself, she feels guilty.

Friends, this path is not sustainable. Tracey and I have experienced firsthand what it looks like for the caregiver to crash because of an empty bucket, and I'm certain this is where Suzanne will land if there's not change.

What's in your bucket?

May 6, 2015
Pure Joy?

"Consider it pure joy, my brothers, whenever you face trials of many kinds, because

you know that the testing of your faith develops perseverance. Let perseverance finish its work so that you may be mature and complete, not lacking anything."
James 1:2–4

Lately, there have been moments of joy in my trials, but *pure* joy? I'm just not there yet. Trials and suffering are tough. They are challenging and can be brutal, which is why, I suppose, they are called trials.

Some of the joys I have experienced recently have included:

Praying for Carolyn
She's my new friend from last week's round of chemo. Cancer is covering Carolyn's stomach. She's not confident her treatment plan is working, or even if she wants to continue. She has a real understanding of what following Jesus looks like and, while she would like to be here for her family, she's ready to put suffering behind her and be with Jesus.

Praying with Miss Daisy
My 88-year-old African-American friend, whose body is failing, is hanging in there. She's a joy to be around (what a great smile she has), but she, too, is ready.

Sharing the love of Jesus with an Uber driver named Fred
Fred is in his 60s, has had a health scare with a throat surgery issue, recently suffered a mild stroke, and is in overall poor health. When I asked where he would be spending eternity, he was honest and answered, "I have no idea." I briefly shared how he could be sure, and I prayed for him, but he wasn't interested and let me know he would figure it out on his own.

Knowing Tracey is Filling Her Bucket
This week, Tracey is in Rosemary Beach, Florida, on an all- expense paid trip with friends. The beach is her happy place, and some friends chose to bless her with this incredible gift, which she sorely needed. As I type this post, I have tears streaming down my face because of this act of generosity. Yes, it's a bit awkward because I'm on a completely booked airplane flight, and I

don't want my seatmates to think I'm emotionally unstable. (My friend Chris Ordway believes when tears are present, the Holy Spirit is nearby and I couldn't agree more.)

Perseverance must finish its work so that you may be mature and complete, not lacking anything.

Look, I'm no theologian, and I could be missing this altogether, but I may be closer to understanding what being "mature and complete and not lacking anything" means.

See, my family and I aren't lacking anything. We have a lovely home and functioning cars. We love each other. We want what's best for each other. We have friends and family who care for us. I get to participate in meaningful work, and I have colleagues I enjoy working with and care about.

However, I'm discovering what really matters is not what we have materially but what we do, what we give, whom we serve, what we share with others, and how we love others.

Honestly, there's nothing in the material realm I need or even want. No, what I really want, what I really yearn for, is to love well, encourage others, and participate in things that matter. There is no joy greater than being involved in these activities.

Maybe this is what James meant by "being mature and complete, not lacking in anything"?

What do you think?

So, what does this have to do with you?

1. *What fills your bucket?*
2. *When was the last time you invested in your personal and spiritual well-being?*
3. *What makes you come alive?*

INVESTING IN MY SON

I WANT JACKSON TO KNOW WHERE HE CAN ALWAYS FIND WISDOM, EVEN IF I'M NOT HERE TO LEAD HIM. WHEN THERE IS UNCERTAINTY AS TO LONGEVITY, YOU LIVE WITH MORE INTENTIONALITY.

"WE'LL DO THAT NEXT YEAR." We no longer say those words in our home. We say *yes* to adventure *now*. Because now is what we have. When there is uncertainty as to longevity, you live with more intentionality.

Jackson was ten years old when I received my cancer diagnosis. Tracey and I were completely clueless about how to include him in the trial we faced. We decided to approach it much like parents handle the sex talk with kids. We told Jackson as much as he wanted to know, but no more.

For one-third of Jackson's life, his dad has wrestled with cancer. Overall, I believe this has been a good thing because it has forced me to be much more intentional with how I invest in my son. Often, kids raised in upscale neighborhoods like ours are brought up with a sense of entitlement. The families I've met who have avoided producing entitled children are intentional about exposing them to other cultures, most often those less fortunate. And kids who have had a trial to deal with while growing up understand life is not all about them.

Kids who have had a trial to deal with while growing up understand life is not all about them.

Even though cancer disrupts, daily life moves along. Early on, I was still working. Jackson was in school, and we were in the regular throes of doing life with chemo treatments. Then and now, there are difficult days, but there are also abundant times of levity.

Following my first surgery and the installation of my first port (the mechanism used to distribute chemotherapy), my doctor discouraged strenuous exercise. Anything more intense than a long walk was forbidden. But I was going stir crazy. One day, I went for a four-mile walk, and on my return, I felt great and decided to run. *What harm could this do?* I increased my pace and leaned into the last mile. Within fifteen yards, my right shoelace wrapped around my left foot and I crashed to the pavement. My sunglasses slid across the road, and my iPhone bounced on the asphalt. My knees were oozing blood, and I was ticked. I remember thinking, *Really, God? I've been through so much. Won't you even allow me to run a mile?*

When I walked into our house, bloodied and pissed, Tracey strongly encouraged me to call my doctor. He told us to head to the Vanderbilt ER immediately, so they could make sure I hadn't done any internal damage.

We picked up Jackson from school and headed to Vanderbilt, where we spent the next several hours. The doctors poked, prodded, and checked everything from a CT scan to—you guessed it—Dr. Slippery Finger.

Tracey and Jackson were in an examination room with me when an attractive female resident entered. She looked at me and quietly asked my family to step into the hallway for a moment.

A few minutes later, after we had discovered there was no rectal bleeding, Jackson and Tracey came back. Jackson immediately asked, "What was that all about, Dad? Why did we have to leave the room?"

Again, Tracey and I had chosen openness with Jackson, so I replied, "Jackson, when someone is sick, doctors must check everything, and I mean *everything*. See, son, I have colon cancer, and the colon is attached to the rectum, so that doctor had to put on rubber gloves and probe my behind to make sure there is no bleeding or additional damage."

At this point, Jackson was standing wide-eyed with his hands on his hips. "Wow, Dad!" he said. "She must really like you!" (No, son, that's not what adults do when they really like each other.)

Cancer is serious business, but whenever I recall this incident, I laugh hard. It's good medicine. (Someone once said anyone who says laughter is the best medicine has apparently not tried morphine, but I digress.)

A few months later, another friend thought I needed to discuss my potential mortality with Jackson. One morning, on the way to school, I said, "Jackson, you know I have a serious disease, and many friends pray for me."

"Yes, Dad," he responded.

"There's a chance this cancer will lead to my death; however, it probably won't be for some time, but it could. Do you ever worry about this?"

"No, Dad, I don't," Jackson replied without missing a beat.

Hmmm, I thought.

Then Jackson piped up, "Dad, you know what I really worry about?"

Thinking we were about to enter a deep, revealing, vulnerable place, I asked, "No, Jackson, what do you worry about?"

"I worry if people keep bringing all of those lasagnas and casseroles, we're gonna run out of space in the freezer for my popsicles."

Often credited to Mark Twain, one of my favorite quotes is, "I am an old man and have known a great many troubles, but most of them never happened."[14] While I was concerned about deep-seated fears in Jackson's life, he was concentrating on the practical—space for popsicles.

In our family, we don't sit around and worry about what could be. It would be easy to live that way, but we find no benefit to it. Instead, we choose to press forward and trust God with our lives.

When we do, there's peace—and lots of laughter.

In our family, we don't sit around and worry about what could be. It would be easy to live that way, but we find no benefit to it. Instead, we choose to press forward and trust God with our lives.

FAITH IN PRACTICE

These days, I'm much more open to the promptings of the Holy Spirit, and I tend to act when prompted. It's normal for Jackson to see me help stranded drivers, pray with strangers, or give a jacket to someone in need. My son is experiencing faith in practice, and that's a good thing.

I believe, where kids are concerned, more is caught than taught. So, while going to church is a good thing, it is exponentially better to *be* the church every day of the week, not just on Sunday.

One day, when Jackson was 13, we were at our local Publix store. As we were walking the soup aisle, we saw a woman who was apparently battling cancer. Her daughter, Jackson's age, had bright pink hair, the color associated with breast cancer awareness. God nudged me to pray for them.

I turned to Jackson and said, "God told me we're supposed to pray for that woman and her daughter." The coolest thing for me is Jackson didn't freak. He responded, "You think so?"

Shoppers packed the soup aisle, so Jackson and I walked around the corner into the open area where the bakery meets the produce. A few minutes later, this mother and daughter emerged around the corner. Immediately Jackson engaged the daughter in conversation, and I said to the mom, "Look, I'm not a pastor, but I believe God wants me to pray with you. See, I'm a fellow cancer patient, and I have made a commitment to God to do whatever he asked me to do. I believe he wants us to pray for you. Are you ok with that?"

About that time, her husband walked up, and I could tell he was a bit irritated and wanted to know what was going on. Again, I shared, "I'm a fellow cancer patient, and I believe God told me to pray for you and your family." The man looked at his wife, and she nodded and said, "It's ok, Honey."

So, in Publix, Jackson and I prayed for that family and asked God to heal the mom. We prayed for strength and asked God to meet their every need. Following our prayer, they said, "Thank you." And we went our separate ways.

Not only was Jackson ok with this activity, but he also participated and acted as if this behavior were everyday stuff. (Believe me, this would have never been the case before my diagnosis because rarely was I in tune with promptings from the Holy Spirit. As a result, my family missed the blessing of engaging and serving others.)

Over the past few years, Jackson has learned to lean into opportunities to help others, myself included. Early on, I remember a day when I was terribly sick. Jackson climbed into bed with me and said, "Dad, grab my hand." He bowed his head and prayed a simple prayer that God would make me feel better. Again, I'm certain this would not have happened before cancer.

Early on, I remember a day when I was terribly sick. Jackson climbed in bed with me and said, "Dad, grab my hand." He bowed his head and prayed a simple prayer that God would make me feel better.

Although Jackson is entirely open to spiritual adventures, he is also in tune with practical realities. One day as we were standing in our family room, he said, "Dad, you can't die."

"Why would you say that?" I asked.

"Well, most every day I'm already late to school. If you die, then Mom will have to get a job, and I'll never get to school on time."

That's when I shared, "Well Jackson, several years ago your mom and I made a wise decision and purchased a life insurance policy. Which means, when I die, your mom will receive a big check so, she won't need to get a job."

Jackson pondered this thought for a few seconds and then, using a hushed voice, he leaned into me, grinned, and asked, "Dad, exactly how much money are we talking?"

BOOKING IT

In the fall of 2015, when the cancer had gotten progressively worse and had become increasingly active in my lungs, I felt a greater sense of urgency and ordered a Bible for Jackson with his name engraved on the leather cover. I told him a gift I ordered for him would arrive any day. He kept asking me what it was. Candidly, I thought Jackson would be disappointed when he discovered the gift was a Bible, but he wasn't. When it arrived, he asked me to fill out the inside page, recording who gave the Bible to him and when. He is so proud of his Bible.

I'm intentional in my interactions with Jackson because I'm not sure how long I will be here. In my opinion, the Bible is the greatest source of wisdom, especially the Book of Proverbs. For years, I've read the daily proverb and have been blown away by the depth of wisdom that emerges. So, while I've read the Book of Proverbs to Jackson, I want him to know where he can always find wisdom, even if I'm not here to lead him.

I've often read to Jackson before bedtime. When he was ten, we began reading Bob Goff's book *Love Does*. Every night, I would ask Jackson what he wanted to read, and every night he would answer, "*Love Does*, Dad."

In February 2014, Jackson, Tracey, and I were in Washington, D.C., at the National Prayer Breakfast. Every year, on the Wednesday before the breakfast, we eat lunch at Buca di Beppo, located just down the block from the Washington Hilton. This day was no different. As we were sitting there, I looked up and noticed Bob seated at a large table across from us. I said to Jackson, "Hey, Buddy, do you know who that man is?"

"No, Dad," Jackson responded.

"That's Bob Goff, son. He wrote the book *Love Does*."

Immediately, Jackson turned and stared at Bob as if he were a rock star.

"Jackson, it's not appropriate to stare at people,"

"Even when they are *that cool*, Dad?"

Bob noticed our exchange and came over, asking if he could sit next to Jackson and, of course, we said, "Sure!"

Jackson turned to Bob and said, "I read your book!"

"Really?" Bob asked. "What was your favorite chapter?"

I thought, *no way will Jackson remember the name of a chapter from a book he read two years ago.* Without missing a beat, Jackson responded, "The first one, 'I'm With You.'"

Bob said, "That chapter is about my friend Randy. Let's give him a call. I know he would love to talk to you." So, Bob dialed his friend and, sure enough, Jackson had a conversation with Randy.

After this exchange, Bob handed Jackson the coolest business card I've ever seen. On the card is printed:

> *Name: Bob Goff*
> *Title: Helpful*
> *Address: Tom Sawyer Island, Disneyland*

As Bob was leaving our table, he asked Jackson, "Why haven't you called me?"

See, Bob included his telephone number in the back of *Love Does* and stated, "I've found that the people in my life who have actually been the most influential have also been the ones who were the most available. If you ever want to talk about any of the ideas in this book that ping you, ... give me a call."[15] So, for everyone who reads his book, Bob is available.

> "I've found that the people in my life who have actually been the most influential have also been the ones who were the most available." Bob Goff

It brings me joy to know Jackson considers Bob Goff his hero and sees him as a cool guy. When I was Jackson's age, I didn't have a lot of heroes of the faith. There were a few, but none like Bob Goff—or the hero I want to be in Jackson's life. (By the way, Jackson called Bob, and he answered.)

If Jackson is the only person who reads *Out of the Blue*, then, for me, it's well worth the effort. It's my prayer that my experiences will help you understand the need for intentionality with your kiddos, the importance of listening to the prompting of the Holy Spirit and that you'll include your kids in your journey—because it's true: Much more is caught than taught.

January 29, 2015
"Dad, his name is Marcelino, and he is my friend."

When Jackson was nine years old, our family led a mission trip to the Dominican Republic (DR). It wasn't a traditional mission trip. Instead, we hosted several families in an incredible home in Casa de Campo and exposed them to real poverty and a few amazing organizations working to serve the poor.

While in the DR, we met the leadership of HOPE International, Cure International, and Healing Waters International. We also had the opportunity to visit their work in the field to see, firsthand, the power and importance of microfinance, medical care in developing regions, and the importance of purified drinking water. It was a life-changing trip on several levels, but what came to mind, as I was walking this morning, is what I learned from my son.

Upon landing in Miami on the journey home, I called my dad and began to share about the incredible experience we had and the fantastic home where we stayed.

I explained the home came fully equipped with a cook and assistant cook, a wait staff, a cleaning crew, a butler, and—it was then Jackson hit me on the shoulder with all his might. BAMM!

Startled, I turned to him and asked, "Hey, Buddy, what was that about?" His response was priceless. He stared at me in anger and said, "Dad, he isn't just a butler. His name is Marcelino, and he is my friend."

Jackson didn't see the staff as staff. He saw them as great people, and they are. Jackson loved to work with them, make them laugh, and hang out with them.

These sweet, hardworking people make about two dollars per day, yet when we were leaving, they threw a party for Jackson and gave him two tee shirts they had pooled their money to purchase. As we drove away from that home, the entire staff was in line waving and yelling goodbye to Jackson. It was a priceless moment.

Do you know the names of the wait staff at your favorite restaurant? How about the security guard at your office building?

Have you taken the time to get to know the names of your Uber drivers?

These are real people who have a lot to offer, and they can become your great friends. This real-life lesson I learned from my son, and it's a great one.

Thanks, Jackson.

"The King will reply, 'Truly I tell you, whatever you did for one of the least of these brothers and sisters of mine, you did for me.'" Matthew 25:40

February 20, 2014
He is Watching

Jackson, my 12-year-old boy/young man, just came in from playing and lay down next to me. He then said, "Dad, hold my hand." I reached out, grabbed his hand, and without saying another word Jackson closed his eyes and prayed, "God, please be with my dad and make him feel better. Amen."

He is watching.

He has seen Tracey and me pray for him, for friends, family members, and strangers.

He is watching, and I couldn't be prouder of my son.

We as parents cannot simply tell our kids to turn to God; we must model that dependence for them.

They are watching.

During tough and trying times, do we become angry and yell? Do we turn to a bottle? Do we turn to comfort food or TV? Or do we turn to the Creator of the Universe?

Whatever you turn to, they are watching.

So, what does this have to do with you?

1. *What are three things your child has caught from you rather than being taught?*

2. *Would your child freak if you prayed for a stranger in the grocery store?*

3. *Who are the people who have had the greatest influence in your life and why?*

SAINT GREG I'M NOT

I WANT TO STAND UP FOR
MYSELF. I WANT TO FIGHT
BACK; I WANT TO SET THINGS
RIGHT. BUT THAT'S NOT
MY JOB.

"YOU'RE A SMARTASS." When a fellow cancer patient said those words to me, he hit the nail on my hard head. I was at Baylor Imaging System in Dallas for a CT scan. Every quarter, I'm examined to determine if the chemo is working.

While I was getting my paperwork from the receptionist, a man who had completed his forms tossed his clipboard over my shoulder. It crash-landed between the young woman and me. Without a word, he turned and walked away.

The receptionist and I exchanged glances, and under her breath, she said, "Well, that was rude." "Yes," I responded. "It was."

Returning to my chair, I took a circuitous route past the impatient patient, and said to him in passing, "What you did back there was rude."

"I may be rude, but you're a smartass," he shot back.

I then responded, "Hmmm, I guess this is how angry old people act."

He stood and asked me if I wanted to take the conversation outside. This man had to be at least 70 years old.

No, I'm not making this up.

My response was to turn away in disgust and

focus on filling out the forms on my clipboard. As I sat there, the Holy Spirit convicted me of causing and escalating a conflict with a fellow patient. And the guy was right; I had acted like a smartass. The nurse called him back for his scan, and I faced the reality that if he returned before I was called back for mine, then I must apologize.

Sure enough, 20 minutes later, he emerged from the back. At that point, I stood up and walked toward him with hand extended to ask for his forgiveness and to confess I was wrong by the way I had approached him.

He immediately responded, "No, my friend. I was wrong. My pastor has been praying with me and challenging me to deal with my anger issues. He refers to me as Peter because I'm the one who seems to always rush into the fight. I'm a retired Dallas police officer. I'm also a Christian, but I have a lot of learning to do."

After confessing that, most of the time, I pray with fellow patients rather than argue, I asked if I could pray for him and his wife. With tears in their eyes, they said they would like that.

Yes, my new friend has anger issues, but I am a smartass. Saint Greg I'm not. Not by a long shot. Why did I approach that man and point out his shortcomings? Because I felt slighted, and I wanted to put him in his place. However, that's not my job.

See, my job is to love, encourage, embrace, pray with, and accept everyone, especially those whom I believe slight me.

Paul said in Romans 12:17-21, "Do not repay anyone evil for evil. Be careful to do what is right in the eyes of everyone. If it is possible, as far as it depends on you, live at peace with everyone. Do not take revenge, my dear friends, but leave room for God's wrath, for it is written: 'It is mine to avenge; I will repay,' says the Lord."

Yes, my new friend has anger issues, but I am a smartass. Saint Greg I'm not. Not by a long shot.

The way we are to live, as followers of Jesus, is entirely opposite of what we would do naturally. In my nature, I want to stand up for myself. I want to fight back; I want to set things right. But that's not my job.

SHE KNOWS

One day, Tracey walked into our family room with tears streaming down her face and said, "Those people who read your blog think you're perfect, but they don't have to live with you."

Tracey's assessment of me is spot on.

In early February of 2015, I was reading the first six chapters of the Book of Exodus. Before you start

thinking I'm a disciplined Bible scholar, allow me to
set you straight. I was reading those six chapters at
one time because I
was already behind
in my read-the-Bi-
ble-in-a-year effort.
This is an annual
failure for me. I can't
tell you how many
times I've started a
Bible-reading pro-
gram and never completed the plan. I guess you
could say I'm a read-the-Bible-in-a-year dropout.
But at least I'm consistent.

> Tracey walked into our
> family room with tears
> streaming down her face
> and said, "Those people who
> read your blog think you're
> perfect, but they don't have
> to live with you."

That day's marathon Bible-reading session
reminded me of how Moses repeatedly said *no* to
God when asked to approach Pharaoh on behalf of
the Israelites: "Who am I that I should go to Pharaoh and bring the Israelites out of Egypt?" (Exodus 3:11). Moses also replied, "Pardon your servant, Lord. I have never been eloquent, neither in
the past nor since you have spoken to your servant.
I am slow of speech and tongue" (Exodus 4:10).

Before my cancer diagnosis, I, like Moses, had
an inferiority complex. For years, I said *no* to any
and every opportunity to speak in public. However,
two hours after I read those Exodus chapters, my
friend Dabbs Cavin called and asked me to keynote

the Arkansas Prayer Breakfast. I would have never even considered such a request before cancer. However, after being frustrated with Moses and writing about him in my journal, I couldn't tell Dabbs *no* even though I could completely relate to Moses and his "never been eloquent" mentality.

So, I waded into the keynote speaker pool—way past my comfort zone—and God showed up at the Arkansas Prayer Breakfast. To my surprise, what God gave me to say resonated deeply with the 400 attendees.

Afterward, Gary Jones asked me to join him for lunch. Gary and I have been friends since our college days. I consider him more of a brother than a friend.

As I arrived at the restaurant, I was on cloud nine. After a morning of facing down my fears and speaking at the breakfast, I felt good about myself. To some extent, I believe it's ok to take pride in an accomplishment—but it's not ok to bask in it. And I was basking. I had sat at the head table with Governor Asa Hutchinson and his wife, Susan, Congressman French Hill, and Senator John Boozman. A guy like me—raised on the other side of the tracks in Southwest Little Rock—had rubbed elbows with the most powerful political figures in Arkansas.

Following the breakfast, there was a long line of people waiting to shake my hand and take pictures with me. Before I could get out of the building, the governor's wife grabbed my hand, looked me in the eyes, and talked with me for 15 minutes. I can't remember what we talked about, but it was intoxicating.

That euphoria leads me to a conversation with Gary.

Gary said, "You did an excellent job, Greg. Your speech was incredible; I'm proud to call you my friend. Last week I spoke with Bill Dillard, Ted Dickey, Kevin Huchingson, and a few others. We all agreed we've never met anyone quite like you."

"Greg, I pray for Tracey every single day. It must be really tough for her to be married to you." Gary Jones

At this point in the conversation, I was about to burst with pride. Then Gary finished his thought, "And because of that fact, you need to know, I pray for Tracey every single day. It must be really tough for her to be married to you."

The popping of my bubble was almost audible. Mentally, I went from, *Bring it on Gary; tell me one more time what a great guy you think I am,* to, *Good grief, he's right.* As an extreme extrovert, there's good stuff that comes with my personality type, but there's loads of junk as well—and Tracey is the one most affected by my dysfunction.

It's important for me to surround myself with those unimpressed by what others are saying about me—an inner circle of family members and friends who aren't swayed by my press clippings. People who have won the right to tell me like it is without pulling any punches.

The truth may sting, but it's medicinal. High-and-mighty King Solomon must have had an honest inner circle, too, because he wrote in Proverbs 27:6, "Wounds from a friend can be trusted, but an enemy multiplies kisses." It's one of my favorite verses because I've lived it.

Interestingly, Gary doesn't remember that conversation, but I will never forget it. I'm thankful for his honesty.

Proverb 27:21 also hits close to home: "The crucible for silver and the furnace for gold, but people are tested by their praise." The human side of me wants to feel as though I'm the most talented writer and speaker in the world. But again, that's not my job. My job is to show up when and where God tells me so he can shine, not me.

OFF TO THE NUNNERY

During a recent treatment, I was dragging my chemo pole down the hall and passed Sister Mary Olivia's treatment room. She's a nun with the Dominican Order in North Nashville. I entered and struck up a conversation. She was extremely encouraging and kind. We prayed together.

A few days later, she sent me an email, inviting me to join her for a tour of the convent, located just north of downtown Nashville, and to participate in their evening prayers. Tracey and I made the trip and were inspired by the facilities, but even more so by the nuns' faithfulness and commitment to Jesus.

Following the time of prayer, we drove off the campus while the sun was gloriously setting in the west. It was a breathtaking environment and a mountain-top experience.

It was 5:45, and we were driving south from Nashville to Brentwood during peak evening traffic. A scant five minutes after saying goodbye to Sister Mary Olivia and the other gracious nuns, I was merging into traffic when a dude driving a huge truck and pulling a camper trailer laid on his horn and shook his fist at me.

Following such a spiritually rewarding experience at the convent, I breathed a soft prayer for this man and yielded to his advancing fury.

Well, not exactly.

Nope, I glanced over my left shoulder and uttered a highly toxic explicative. (I won't go into detail because you might not read the rest of my book.) After my outburst of anger, I pressed the gas pedal to the floor, leaving the man exactly where he deserved to be—in my dust. Alas, this is a sad-but-true story of a day in the life of road warrior Greg Murtha.

No one has ever called me Saint Greg while I was driving. Jackson will quickly attest to this fact. Recently, I was driving him to school when a man darted out of the line of traffic in front of us and came perilously close to causing an accident. I laid on the horn and uttered, "What an idiot!"

Jackson responded, "It's interesting, Dad. When you do something because you're avoiding lining up in traffic like all the other sheep, you think it's ok. But when someone else does it to you, he's an idiot."

Ouch. But Jackson's right. Candidly, there's a reason I don't have the *Ichthus* image on my car bumper. The way I behave behind the wheel needs to be modified, not emulated. I want to be first in traffic, but my mantra should be: "That's not my job or my right."

Nope, Saint Greg I'm not. But here's the great news: I'm forgiven, and as time passes, I'm getting better. Better at realizing my shortcomings, better at asking forgiveness, and better at attempting to follow Jesus' model of how to love and lead. Jesus offers a better way, and while

The way I behave behind the wheel needs to be modified, not emulated.

I falter daily, I want to live his way the rest of my one-and-only life.

December 15, 2016
His name was Fred Cobb, but really, he was Jesus.

Fred was a newspaper salesman. He was poor, but he always had a smile. Every day, Fred wore his "I Love Jesus" hat. Often, he was at the north end of Franklin Road, smiling and waving. And just as often, I avoided him.

I am a goat.

It's not just Fred. It's anyone I'm inconvenienced by who requires me to rummage through my car for the cash needed to buy a *Contributor* paper I never read.

I mean, it's not my fault this guy is on the streets. Right?

This morning I read that Fred died. I also read an article about him in *Southern Exposure Magazine* that is ironically dated December 15, 2015, one year ago today.

Reading the article, I learned Fred had been a Service Merchandise employee and was a good guy. Then tragedy struck. His wife discovered she had cancer, and eight months later, she was gone. That's when Fred checked out and ended up on the streets.

There's a passage in Matthew 25:32-46 worth reading. It's about sheep who embrace interruptions and goats who do not. Check it out.

How often was Jesus interrupted in his daily life and what did he do about it? Well, he didn't look the other way. Nope, Jesus treated them like valued human beings. He entered their world, understood their pain, and met their needs.

Interestingly, why was Jesus so open to the interruptions? Why wasn't he more driven, like me, to accomplish goals? I mean, didn't he know he only had three years from age 30 to 33 to fulfill his earthly mission?

Maybe embracing interruptions *was* his mission? Maybe if we're not allowing ourselves to be interrupted, then we aren't following Jesus?

This morning I live in regret. For years, I looked the other way when I saw Fred, and for this I'm sorry.

December 15, 2015
Convicted in the Chick-fil-A
Drive-Thru

Yesterday, at 12:30 pm, I was taking Jackson through a Chick-fil-A Drive-Thru to grab a quick lunch.

Attempting the drive through at that time of day is akin to driving in Delhi, India, with cars coming from three directions, all trying to merge into one line.

Three lanes were seamlessly merging into one when a soccer mom in a black SUV aggressively moved forward, honking her horn to get through. I'm a man of order, rights, and justice–and the way I saw it, what she was doing was wrong. So, I attempted, in haste, to slide my loafer on so I could exit my vehicle and enact justice by standing in front of her car and letting the other cars merge, in order.

However, before I could get my shoe on, this mom passed the drive-thru line and parked. See, she wasn't breaking in line; she was merely attempting to avoid the line so she could take her kids inside.

Jackson sat quietly, watching this whole scene play out. Then he reminded me: "Dad, a fool gives full vent to his anger." See, we've been reading through the Book of Proverbs on a consistent basis, and Solomon equated anger with being a fool.

Boom! I was busted. I was angry with this woman—wrongfully angry, I might add. And I had a quick response to the Holy Spirit sitting next to me in Nike basketball shorts. "Jackson, that was not *full vent* to my anger. That was probably a 25 percent vent."

His response, "That's ok, Dad, but now you're justifying your sin."

Are you kidding me? Is this my 13-year-old? Did he listen when we read the Proverbs? Did he correctly apply a verse to a situation where I was wrong? Did God use this young man to convict me of sin?

Yes. He. Did.

I couldn't be prouder of Jackson. He's listening.

Are you spending time in the Proverbs on a consistent basis? Allow me to encourage you to read one per day. There are 31 chapters in the Book of Proverbs, so it is easy to read the Proverb of the Day. Today is Proverbs 15, and it's so rich. Share these proverbs with your kids as well. They may use what they learn to keep you from embarrassing yourself. Mine did.

So, what does this have to do with you?

1. *When was the last time you went into a situation thinking, If God doesn't show up, I'm dead meat?*

2. *When was the last time you were prompted to apologize for something you had said or done? Did you?*

3. *Who are the people in your life who will flat out tell you the truth?*

CHURCH OF THE BENT AND BRUISED

IF YOU FOLLOW GOD'S PLAN BY BEING THE CHURCH WHEREVER YOU ARE, WHO KNOWS? MAYBE GOD WILL USE YOU AND YOUR RAGTAG GROUP OF FRIENDS TO CHANGE THE WORLD.

EVER ATTENDED AN ALCOHOLICS ANON-YMOUS (AA) MEETING? To me, an AA meeting is closer to what God intended when he formed the church than what most of us experience on Sunday mornings.

I have childhood memories of getting dressed in my Sunday clothes and sitting with a group of people who didn't talk about the Herculean effort it took to get to church on time. No one mentioned the yelling and consternation occurring in most cars on the way to the place where we were expected to appear as though we were shiny happy people with no real needs, people who truly had it all together.

Compare that to an AA meeting, where everybody arrives admitting they are bent and bruised. They all lean on one another for support, accountability, and acceptance. And they know they cannot make it without relying on a Higher Power. In the institutional church, so dominant in the good old USA, we've been made to feel we must act as if we have it all together, which is inauthentic at best and a complete and utter lie at worst.

Groucho Marx once said, "Please accept my resignation. I don't want to belong to any club that will accept people like me as a member."[16]

If the real heart of the institutional church reflected Groucho's mindset, there would be far fewer problems. We would accept the fact we're all broken and in desperate need of grace. We would be welcoming to all. We would walk, limp, or crawl in the door as what Brennan Manning called Ragamuffins—the broken, bent, bruised, and bedraggled. We would be much less apt to throw stones. We would be much more likely to encourage our fellow sinners by offering them support, accountability, and an introduction to the ultimate Higher Power—Jesus Christ.

If the real heart of the institutional church reflected Groucho's mindset, there would be far fewer problems.

At the beginning of his seminal book, *The Ragamuffin Gospel*, Manning defined his target audience:

> *This book is not for the superspiritual.*
> *It is not for red-hot zealots who boast with*
> *the rich young ruler of the Gospels, 'All these*
> *commandments I have kept from my youth.'*
> *It is not for the complacent who hoist over*
> *their shoulders a tote bag of honors, diplo-*
> *mas, and good works, actually believing they*
> *have it made. It is not for the legalists who*
> *would rather surrender control of their souls*
> *to rules than run the risk of living in union*
> *with Jesus.*[17]

Manning went on to say,

> *If anyone is still reading along, The Raga-*
> *muffin Gospel was written for the bedrag-*
> *gled, beat-up, and burnt-out . . .*

> *It is for the bent and bruised who feel their*
> *lives are a grave disappointment to God . . .*

> *The Ragamuffin Gospel is a book I wrote for*
> *myself and anyone who has grown weary*
> *and discouraged along the way.*[18]

Ah, *The Ragamuffin Gospel* is for me—bent, bedraggled, and bruised Greg Murtha. The truth is, I think the *Ragamuffin* attitude is attractive to all. I've shed many a tear reading Manning's book because it reminds me Jesus came to Hotel Earth for people like me. I'm accepted and loved just the way I am. And I thank God for that!

I recently purchased *The Ragamuffin Gospel* for a friend who is tired of trying to measure up. She fled the institutional church long ago. Recently she texted me this note:

> *Greg, I love this book already. I love how*
> *Manning says, 'It is for the bent and*
> *bruised who feel their lives are a grave*

> *disappointment to God!' Tears are stream-*
> *ing down my face. I'm the weird girl crying*
> *in the corner of Starbucks. That's how I feel*
> *most days.*

Did you catch that? She was vulnerable. She shared how she feels most days. And she's in need of love and acceptance without a lot of rules attached. Like many, she feels she'll never measure up to the standards of the institutional church. But you know what? Jesus would tell her otherwise. He would pull up a chair in that corner of Starbucks and tell her he loves her just the way she is. No need to dress to impress. No need to pretend.

BE THE CHURCH

Sadly, the institutional church has become more like a country club. Programs and activities are created to keep people occupied, entertained, and out of trouble. A church in my neck of the woods recently spent megabucks on a sports center— along with a coffee shop far bigger and better than any Starbucks I've ever entered. I don't see Jesus in

Sadly, the institutional church has become more like a country club. Programs and activities are created to keep people occupied, entertained, and out of trouble.

this at all. Nor do I see this approach to church in the Book of Acts.

When asked by the Pharisees, "Why do you eat and drink with tax collectors and sinners?" Jesus replied, "It is not the healthy who need a doctor, but the sick. I have not come to call the righteous, but the sinners" (Mark 2:17).

If we spend all our time (and money) on a church campus, drinking premium coffee and playing ball in a sports complex with people who already call themselves Christians, then we have a lot less time and money to be with those who need a physician—the bent and bruised Jesus came to serve and save.

The USA church of today owns a lot of prime real estate, but I fear it has walled itself in. At least, that's the way I see things after being out in the real world for five years.

The bent and bruised aren't sipping premium espresso in a church's coffee shop or shooting hoops in its sports complex. Nope, the bent and bruised are crying in the corner of Starbucks because they don't think they are worthy of forgiveness. The bent and bruised are standing in line at the pharmacy, trying to figure out how to buy medicine and groceries. The bent and bruised are wearing hats to cover bald heads and wrapping gauze around protruding tumors, always conscious of those who stare and then turn away.

The bent and bruised feel alone.

The bent and bruised aren't looking for someone to invite them to church. They are looking for someone to *be the church.*

The most worshipful experiences I've had during the past five years have not been in church buildings. Instead, one was at a bar in Beaver Creek, Colorado, with someone who felt defeated and ashamed. Another happened at a friend's home in Evergreen, Colorado, where Tracey and I met a husband and wife who had lost everything in a fire and were forever changed—for the better. Another sacred moment happened in a hardware store when three strangers held hands and prayed for strength to walk the uneven path of chronic illness.

> The bent and bruised aren't looking for someone to invite them to church. They are looking for someone to be the church.

These weren't times when I was *in a church.* These were times when I *was the church.*

Often, I get to come alongside fellow patients who need love, support, and encouragement. In well over five years of being in hospital waiting rooms, I've approached dozens of people with the purpose of encouraging them, sharing their load, and offering a prayer. It's not uncommon for me to hear the question, "Are you a pastor?" to which I reply, "No, I'm a businessman and a fellow cancer patient, but why should pastors have all the fun?" It's an absolute blast for me to come alongside people God leads me to and do what he asks. It's no more complex than that.

Here's the deal: We make our faith in Jesus, and how we practice our religion, far too complex. I've discovered if I do three things daily, then everything else seems to take care of itself.

1. Read my Bible. Most every day I start with reading a chapter from the Book of Proverbs, a deep well of wisdom. Think about it. Daily, I get to sit at the feet of Solomon, the wisest man who ever lived. That's a gift, not an arduous task. Try it!

2. Pray. When I pray, I write in my journal whatever God brings to my mind. Often, I create a list of things for which I'm thankful. I write prayers for myself. I write prayers for others. Then I listen. What I'm trying to improve on is making sure my time of prayer includes more gratefulness and listening than asking.

3. Do what God says. Following time in Scripture and prayer, I attempt to slow down enough to hear the still, small voice of the Holy Spirit. Then I simply do whatever he asks. When I live this way, I'm able to join him in his bigger story. The way I see things, this is the role of a lifetime.

This three-step approach to faith is as complicated as my religion gets. The hardest part of this equation is the slowing down aspect because I have an ingrained tendency to believe if something is going to happen, then I must make it happen. But God is teaching me that's not how it works.

BEATING GOD AT HIS GAME

Recently, I was in Chicago for the Willow Creek Leadership Summit. My friend Jossy Chacko, the founder of Empart (a community transformation organization focused in Asia), was a keynote speaker. He communicated leadership principles that were well received by the audience of 275,000 leaders worldwide. However, what truly captured my attention was what he said in a short interview segment following his keynote address.

> "How could two companies from the West beat God at his game? The brand names Coca-Cola and McDonald's are better known around the globe than Jesus. And we had a 2,000-year head start!" Jossy Chacko

Jossy asked a profound question, "How could two companies from the West beat God at his game? See, the brand names Coca-Cola® and McDonald's® are better known around the globe than Jesus. And we had a 2,000-year head start! Do you think this is because God is a bad businessman and that he has a bad plan? Or could it be, those of us who call ourselves Christians haven't done a good job of following his plan?"

Hmm, following God's plan. Not ours. Sounds familiar, doesn't it?

Eighteen years ago, when Jossy launched Empart to set in motion community transformation in India, he used the Book of Acts as his management guide and strategic plan. The leadership of the ministry and the community workers who do the heavy lifting are required to read the Book of Acts once a month. That way, God's plan is always at the forefront of their minds.

Empart has helped transform 22,000 communities in 18 years and trained 7,700 workers. Community workers must be focused externally on meeting the needs of their community, such as serving orphaned street kids and the mentally unstable on the edges of society. They must reach out with a message of hope, meet weekly in homes, and engage in the lives of others on a consistent basis. As community leaders, they are not told what to do. Instead, they are encouraged to listen to God—and then do what he asks them to do.

Empart believers are being the hands and feet of Jesus by meeting the needs of those in their sphere of influence. Notice I didn't say they go to church or they have a premium coffee shop or professional-level sports courts. No, they are being the church, which I believe is what God intended and where true life is found. Frankly, don't take my word for it. Read the Book of Acts.

Does the Empart approach sound anything like what you experience on a weekly basis in your home church or the church of your youth? If so, bravo! But I would say this is the exception, not the rule. Is there a church in your community serving the broken and opening its doors to the bent and bruised? If so, don't walk to join them. *Run to join them.*

> Is there a church in your community serving the broken and opening its doors to the bent and bruised? If so, don't walk to join them. *Run to join them.*

Here's what I've discovered as I've been forced to slow down and simply do what God asks me to do. He doesn't use my abilities as a strategic planner or as an experienced businessman. To the contrary, he more often leverages my weakness rather than my strengths for his glory. Never in the five-plus years of my hospital-based ministry to fellow cancer patients has God used my ability to draft a business plan or create a marketing strategy. Instead, I share the burden others have been tapped to carry. I know how heavy that burden feels. I know where the bruises are. Being a business leader in this setting hinders more than helps. Being the church? Well, that works wonders.

See, I was public school educated in the state of Arkansas. I didn't graduate from a prestigious boarding school or university. Heck, I didn't even make top grades at the University of Arkansas. But God uses the simple to confound the wise. And this simple guy has a blast engaging in life this way.

Jim Denison gets this simplicity. In the May 4, 2017, issue of "The Denison Forum," he put it this way:

> *God so often uses small places for big purposes. He used the bush in the wilderness to call Moses; he used a slingshot to defeat a giant and elevate a king; he used a cave on a prison island to give the world his Revelation. First Corinthians 1:26-29 comes to mind:*
>
> *'Not many of you were wise by human standards; not many were influential; not many were of noble birth. But God chose the foolish things of the world to shame the wise; God chose the weak things of the world to*

shame the strong. God chose the lowly things
of this world and the despised things—and
the things that are not—to nullify the things
that are, so that no one may boast before
him.'[19]

What did each of the small places Denison listed have in common? The individuals involved were doing God's work in God's way. They weren't seeking to entertain the wealthy and ensure comfort with contrived programs and grand buildings.

Dietrich Bonhoeffer didn't pull any punches regarding his beliefs about what the church is:

'The church represents that gracious realm
of God where sinners are welcomed, the
wounded are healed, the oppressed are set
free, and the poor receive the good news of
the gospel.' In The Communion of Saints,
Bonhoeffer defined the church as 'Christ
existing as community.' He believed that
through the work of the Holy Spirit, Christ
actually takes form in this community as it
lives for others. Christ is revealed not just
through the preached Word and the admin-
istered sacraments, but through the Chris-
tian community itself.[20]

Maybe that's why I feel so alive when I'm brushing elbows with bruised, bent, and broken people who have chosen to live vulnerable, authentic, messy lives instead of putting on masks, dressing up, and trying to act as if they have it together. It's like an AA meeting on steroids. It's real and liberating to be a ragamuffin.

> I feel so alive when I'm brushing elbows with bruised, bent, and broken people. It's like an AA meeting on steroids.

Allow me to encourage you to slow down and follow Jesus wherever he leads. Look for the bent and bruised and reach out to them. Embrace friends who desire to live with authenticity, friends who provide support and accountability, friends who accept you just as you are. Ragamuffin friends who know they cannot make it without relying on the Higher Power—Jesus of Nazareth.

You may be able to locate these friends in a building of people who meet every Sunday, but maybe not. However, if you follow God's plan by being the church wherever you are, who knows? Maybe God will use you and your ragtag group of friends to change the world.

May 15, 2016
Molly and Mom

Today I began my 52nd round of chemotherapy. My morning began with the following schedule:

7:00 a.m. labs
8:00 a.m. doctor's visit
9:00 a.m. chemotherapy

Following my doctor's visit, I was running late.

It was 8:50, and I needed to retrieve my chemo pump from my car. I also needed to grab some breakfast, which is a ten-minute walk each way to the Au Bon Pain in Vanderbilt hospital. As it was, I was already going to be at least 30 minutes late to my appointment in the infusion room.

As I was walking through the waiting room, I saw a 30-something woman with long blonde hair holding two documents, one pink and one white. Seeing those documents informed me she was a fellow cancer patient. As I walked past her, I noticed she had a tear in her eye.

I knew I was supposed to stop and pray with her, but I was late. So, I kept walking.

Ok, God. I have a stomachache. A few more steps. *You know I'm late.* A few steps. *I'm not feeling well.* A few more steps. And then, I stopped. I had made a commitment to act when prompted by the Holy Spirit, so I turned around and went to her.

As I approached, I noticed the one tear had multiplied, and she was attempting to hold back the floodgates.

Me: Hello. God told me I am supposed to pray for you. Are you ok with that?

Molly: Yes, I would like it a lot.

Me: Are you a cancer patient?

Molly: Yes, I am.

Me: Me too. Today is my 52nd round of chemo. I've been at this since January 2012.
Molly: I'm sorry to hear that.

Me: What's your name?

Molly: My name is Molly. My mom died today. She had the same form of cancer I have.

Me: I'm so sorry to hear that. Just yesterday I was talking to a friend about how thankful I am that my mom, whose name is Mallie, is in heaven. See, my mom had cancer too (the same form I have), and the last six months of her life were a beating. She suffered too long, and I can't tell you how grateful I am she is in a place where there is no suffering, no chemo, and no radiation.

Molly: My mom is a believer too, and I know she is with Jesus.

We bowed our heads, I placed my hand on her shoulder, and I thanked God for our moms. I thanked him they were with him and no longer suffering. I prayed for Molly and her battle and asked God to comfort her on this difficult day.

When I said, "Amen," Molly grabbed me and hugged me as she wept. She thanked me for my prayer and told me she would be praying for me.

I'm learning that being present in the moment is what is important. Being the church wherever I am—that's what matters. Listening to the prompting of the Holy Spirit is paramount to living a life of adventure. If I had kept going, I would have missed the highlight of my day.

Finally, I can't tell you how thankful I am that I have no question where my sweet mom is enjoying eternity. She loved my siblings and me, she loved others, and she loved Jesus. As those of you who were her friends know, she was an incredible woman through and through.

Join me in praying for Molly. Today is a tough one for her.

April 19, 2016
Jaggie Love

So, I'm sitting on the front porch listening to the Give Me Jesus station on our SONOS system. My journal is in my lap, and my Bible is nearby. My plan is to start the day by reading my Bible, writing prayers in my journal, and trying to listen to God.

However, God may have other plans?

When I was about to start writing, our dog Jaggie trots up and places his head near my hand. Yes, he is begging for some affection. What would make him happy is a hand on his head and a few words of affirmation.

Interesting parallel.

While I was in the process of approaching my Master, Jaggie did the same thing. While I have a pen, my journal and Bible, coffee, and music, Jaggie just comes to me as he is.

For Jaggie, it's simple.

Frankly, I believe we humans overcomplicate this faith/religion thing. We feel we must go to a place, wear the appropriate clothing, behave a certain way, read the right book, have our stuff together, etc. But I'm certain God will accept us as we are, wherever we are. We just need to show up. Like Jaggie.

Jaggie knows I love him, and he just wants to be near me. He obeys me because he knows I want what's best for him and he is better for it.

Father, help me to approach you in the same simple manner as Jaggie. Help me to remember you love me unconditionally and all I need to do is show up and hang out with you, just as I am. Help me to remember that you want what's best for my family and me.

May we all remember this lesson and realize Jesus came for a relationship with us, not to create some religious system with arduous requirements that would be impossible to adhere to.

Father, help me to remember I just need to place my head near your hand and trust you love me like I love Jaggie. Help us all to keep it simple.

Amen.

So, what does this have to do with you?

1. *How do you react when you encounter a stranger who appears to need help?*

2. *When was the last time you were in church? When was the last time you were the church?*

3. *What gets in your way of being the church to the bent and bruised?*

THE ADVENTURE OF YES

IT'S NOT JUST ABOUT ME. IT'S ABOUT YOU. IT'S ABOUT ALL OF US.

WHEN SOMETHING BRINGS ME JOY, I share that product or experience with others. Here are a few examples:

Norah Jones. When she first emerged on the scene, I loved her music and bought her record for numerous friends. It is so good; I had to share it.

The Boys in the Boat by Daniel James Brown. A few years ago, I read this book. It mesmerized me—to the point I've purchased at least 20 copies for friends.

The Ragamuffin Gospel by Brennan Manning. This book hit bookstore shelves in 1990, but recently I gave away yet another copy. (Really, I've lost count.) If you haven't read it, then do yourself a favor and order it immediately.

The Way of Brokenness by Anne Voskamp. I discovered this gem in early 2017. It has helped me as I've walked the path of suffering. I've shared it with others who are traversing rocky roads. It gets to the heart of all things broken.

If I'm so passionate about a couple of books and records, then shouldn't I be even more passionate about telling people where I've found life, the abundant life?

Lauren Daigle. I was late to the party on this one. Lauren's debut record has been out for several years. After discovering it, I gave a dozen iTunes gifts of her album "How Can It Be" to friends across the country, and I'm certain to give more.

All this joy sharing begs the question, *If I'm so passionate about a couple of books and records, then shouldn't I be even more passionate about telling people where I've found life, the abundant life?*

In blog posts over the past five years, I've shared the joy I've received in slowing down enough to hear the still, small voice of the Holy Spirit and saying *yes* to whatever he prompts me to do. When I say *yes* to God, I make friends, serve others, experience joy, and embrace the adventure of a lifetime. I want everyone to have this experience because this is not just about me. It's about you. It's about all of us.

When I first went to work with Bob Buford at the Halftime Institute, I asked him, "If this organization is successful, what will it look like in 20 years?" He responded, "I will consider it a success if, as a direct result of our work, we have ten black-and-white glossies hanging in the lobby with brief stories of how God is using these people to change the world."

I'm proud to say there aren't ten black-and-white glossies hanging in a lobby. Instead, there are hundreds, if not thousands, of individuals who have engaged in service to others because of the Halftime Institute. These people said *yes*—and God is using them to change the world—one life at a time.

Much like Bob, I believe this book, my speaking, and my blogging efforts will have been successful if individuals in my sphere of influence truly slow down, listen to the still small voice of the Holy Spirit, and do what he asks them to do.

> "I have learned that I will not change the world. Jesus will do that. I can, however, change the world for one person." Katie J. Davis

Following are a few examples of notes I've received over the past five years from individuals who said *yes* to the promptings of the Holy Spirit, leaned into it, and, as a result, got to watch God at work in the lives of individuals, most of whom were total strangers.

There's nothing earth shattering here, or is there? As Katie J. Davis, missionary and mom to 14 Ugandan girls, said in her *New York Times* bestselling book *Kisses from Katie,* "I have learned that I will not change the world. Jesus will do that. I can, however, change the world for one person . . . So, I keep stopping and loving one person at a time. Because this is my call as a Christian." [21]

On April 24, 2017, I posted on Facebook that my birthday was the next day. Instead of cards and gifts, I challenged my friends with the following:

Start your day by:
1. Reading God's Word. Read Proverbs 25 and ask God to share his wisdom with you.
2. Praying. Thank God for your blessings, share your prayer request with him, and then just sit and listen.
3. Listening and acting. Move slowly enough tomorrow to hear God's still, small voice and do what he asks you to do.

I hope this collection of notes I received will encourage you to stop and love one person at a time. It's my prayer you'll join Katie Davis, my new friends, and me on this grand adventure of a lifetime.

I did it, Greg! But not as you instructed. I got a few hours into my day and wasn't feeling inspired, more a bit lost. So, I pulled into the parking lot where there are all kinds of stores, including Dunkin Donuts. I read the Proverb of the day, and then I prayed for a sign from God of how he wanted me to serve him best. Prayed for you too! I was a bit teary-eyed when I went into the coffee shop because there was no one in there to buy coffee for. I walked back out to my car and saw a firetruck parked in the lot. So, I found the crew in Qdoba eating lunch, having already paid. I bought a gift certificate and walked over to their table. Told them a bit about you and what you asked all of us to do. They were shocked, and said thank you to me and to say thanks to you.

Greg, I honestly feel a connection to Jesus. And to you! I hope you have the most amazing birthday today! I pray you have many more!

My favorite human—that's you!

Alicia

Hi Greg,

Thanks to you, last night when the young woman next to me on the plane was in tears due to turbulence, I held her hand and asked if I could pray for her. She agreed, and I did so with no concern for who else might hear.

Thanks for speaking the truth, which gave me God's courage to do this. I continue to pray for your healing and your ministry.

Diana

Dear Greg,

I don't know why any of us are here, while some aren't. I do know you inspire me.

Last week when I left work, a woman was sitting behind a bush in the shade. It was a hot day, and usually, I would have minded my own business and kept walking. But because of you (God's messenger), I stopped and asked if she was ok. Did she need anything, perhaps a ride?

This is scary, putting yourself out there, helping or being willing to help others. I was petrified. She was surprised and moved by my questions and suggestions. She didn't need anything, and her ride was on the way. She was just resting and waiting, but she smiled so big and was genuinely happy that I had asked. We talked for a few moments, and I was sure she was ok.

Seems so simple a thing to do, but the fear that another human would need my help, outside of my normal hospital duties, was terrifying—my time, my car, sharing my soul. Now, I wish she had needed something, but we both walked away, smiling and reassured in humankind, better for the interaction. She extended her blessings over me, and I did the same for her.

You inspire me.

In the past, I wouldn't have said a word to the woman by the bush. These are baby steps for me, but steps nonetheless. I am a work in progress.

I want to be a better person and an extension of God's will. Your stories and motivation help me find my footing, baby steps. You and your interactions with others continue to

inspire me, and I just wanted to let you know.
Thank you—and please keep sharing. I will
continue to pray for you and your family.

April

Greg,

I was at the Nissan dealership getting my
car serviced today. I started talking to a guy
next to me, Don. We talked a while, and
then he told me his wife has cancer. Interest-
ing, my mom has cancer so I could relate.

We talked about her treatment. As we spoke,
a lady walked in behind us, heard us talking,
and said, "I am a cancer patient." I turned
to speak to her and saw a sweet, smiling
African-American woman named Josephine
(Jo). Interesting, her oncologist was also one
of my mom's doctors.

For the next few minutes, I listened to Jo
talk to Don about his wife. Then my friend
Chuck texted me; he was there to pick me
up, but I remembered your boldness.

Don and Linda have been married for 50 years. By the time doctors found cancer in Linda's kidney, the disease had migrated to her brain. Jo has breast cancer.

Before I left, I walked around, sat by Jo, and asked her if I could pray for her. She said yes and grabbed my hand. Before I left the waiting area, I had the privilege of praying for Jo, Linda, and Don aloud.

Frankly, I would NEVER have been this bold if you had not set the example of what Christ would want me to do in this situation.

You are making a difference, Greg. Thank you for being Christ's messenger on earth for those who are suffering. Thank you for being the man you are. Thank you for your boldness!

David

Greg,

I thought of you today, even though we have never met. I have read your stories about listening to God when he prompts you to act. I've struggled with that and ignored it many times. Cause let's be honest; sometimes it's just awkward.

I have twin grandbaby boys that are in the hospital with RSV, and one has pneumonia. It's a scary time because they are preemies.

I'm here in Texas helping my son and daughter-in-law with the babies. This morning, I was at Einstein Bagel, waiting on my order. I saw a big group of men, and as I walked by, I heard one of them saying something about Scripture. I felt like God told me to ask them to pray for my grandsons. But I was like, Lord, that is super awkward. Why are you asking me to do this?

Keep in mind, I am new to this, and I was struggling. I looked over, and there were three women at a table with their Bibles out. I feel like God was saying, Ok, how about them?

I'm like, Ok, Lord I can do this. I walked to their table and admitted how awkward I felt. But I felt like the Lord led me to them. I told them our situation, and they offered me a seat, and we held hands, and they prayed for my precious babies.

I just wanted you to know this. I want so much to be obedient and respond when prompted. Those ladies were gracious and loving. The prayer they prayed gave me so much peace that our Heavenly Father loves us and is victorious in all things!

Debbie

Friends, when was the last time God interrupted you out of the blue to do something for someone? God is offering you and me opportunities to join him on the grand adventure. Whether it's praying for someone, asking others to pray for you, buying someone a beverage, or whatever, the adventure of yes is right

> God is offering you and me opportunities to join him on the grand adventure. The adventure of yes is right in front of us every day.

in front of us every day. Katie Davis understands the immense value of small, everyday things.

> *Over time, though, the small changes add up. Sometimes they even transform cities and nations, and yes, the world.* [22]

Sure, it will be awkward at first, but when God prompts, please do what he asks. God is not a kill-joy—just the opposite. He wants what's best for us—the adventure of *yes*!

Join my new friends and me in our quest to follow Jesus and the promptings of the Holy Spirit. Who knows, maybe God could use us—a rag-tag group of people from various walks of life—to change the world?

August 26, 2016
A Kind Deed for Someone

This afternoon I was reading the obituary of a childhood friend, Denny Sims. At the bottom was a line that read, "In lieu of flowers, it was Denny's wish that you do a kind deed for someone."

Interesting.

It has been my experience that listening to the still, small voice in your heart and doing what it says is a reward. Often, when I say *yes* to what I call "the prompting of the Holy Spirit," I'm blessed more than the person receiving the kind deed.

It's a win, win, win.
It's a win for me as it is a blessing to be a blessing.
It's a win for the person on the receiving end of the kind deed.
It's a win for the kingdom as we are an extension of the God of the universe by being the hands and feet of Jesus.

How cool would it be if we (Christians) were known by our kindness, by our acts of service, by how we stand up for those who cannot stand for themselves—instead of what we're against?

Will you join me? Look around. I'm certain, if you look, you'll see some way you can be a blessing to others. When you do, please send me a message and let me know you've embraced the adventure of *yes*.

Life is short. Make it better by loving and serving others.

"For we are God's handiwork, created in Christ Jesus to do good works, which God prepared in advance for us to do."
Ephesians 2:10

April 24, 2017
The Risk of Playing It Safe
Often, I wonder which is greater: the risk of saying *yes* when prompted by the Holy Spirit to join God on an adventure–or the risk of ignoring his promptings, the risk of playing it safe?

Our Heavenly Father is a God of adventure, a God of love, a God of provision. He is a God who can do whatever he wants. He doesn't need our involvement; he just happens to be so generous he invites us to join him on the journey and to share in the joy that comes from partnering with him.

Nine years ago, my friend JT Olson had an idea of how God could use his life experiences to serve Christian families who had the desire to adopt but not the resources. To say JT is uniquely gifted for the role he was dreaming of is an understatement.

JT had the idea, but not the resources. And he had five kids, three of whom were approaching college age. He also had a mortgage and a boatload of responsibilities. But God gave him a great idea.

Last week, I had the privilege of introducing JT to a group of friends in Little Rock. He shared his story of how God took the fact he was orphaned as a 12-years-old. A widow embraced JT and his siblings. As an adult, JT adopted a beautiful girl and called her Grace. He knew how to recruit and motivate teams, something he had done professionally for almost two decades.

God uniquely equipped him to start the Both Hands Foundation (bothhands.org), and JT said yes. If JT had said no, then I'm certain no one would have thought any less of him. But he said yes. He trusted God, exercised faith, and went for it.

Fast forward nine years after JT and his family initially stepped out in faith. What does the scorecard look like? Was it worth the risk? What do you think?

Both Hands Foundation
Founded in 2008
Orphans Closer to Home - 797
Dollars Raised (for Christian families with the desire to adopt) - $7.6 Million
Widows Served - 734
Projects in 42 States – 663
Olson Kids Graduated from College – 2
Olson Kids Pursuing a Master's Degree – 1
Olson Kids Currently Enrolled in College – 1
Olson Mortgage Met - Every month

I am thankful JT, Sara, and their kids risked it for the kingdom.

"Religion that God our Father accepts as pure and faultless is this: to look after orphans and widows in their distress and to keep oneself from being polluted by the world." James 1:27

So, what does this have to do with you?

1. *What keeps you from responding when God prompts you to help someone?*
2. *When was the last time you experienced the joy that comes from focusing on others rather than yourself?*
3. *What would dramatically change in your life if you said, "Yes, God, I'm all in!"?*

MY FINAL CHAPTER

WHEN I CHECK OUT OF HOTEL
EARTH, PLEASE DON'T SAY, "GREG
LOST HIS BATTLE WITH CANCER."
THAT WILL NOT BE THE TRUTH. NO,
WHEN THAT TIME COMES, WHEN I
GET TO THE FRONT OF THE LINE, IT
WILL BE A POINT IN TIME WHEN I
HAVE NEVER BEEN MORE ALIVE,
AND IT WILL BE AN EPIC WIN!

"GREG, THERE'S NO CURE FOR WHAT YOU HAVE." My oncologist's words didn't surprise me, but here are some that might surprise you: *There's no cure for what you have either.* Like me, you're terminal. I may be closer to the front of the line than you—but maybe not. The truth is nobody leaves Hotel Earth alive. God did not design our bodies to last forever. And they don't. Some of us take a long, hard beating on the way to the front of the line; others check out without notice.

In early February 2017, I read the obituary of an acquaintance from Little Rock. Chris loved Jesus. He loved and honored his wife. Chris adored his family. He was a servant to friends and well respected in the community. On his final day, Chris served his teenaged daughter breakfast in bed; his last activity on earth was delivering a wheelchair to a friend in need.

Two hours later, he was standing in the presence of Jesus.

Chris had no idea he would check out that day; however, it appears he left this world with no regrets. His outlook on life reminds me of the verve of William Wallace (*Braveheart*): "Every man dies. Not every man really lives."[23]

During his short time on earth, Chris *really lived*. But from what I have observed, his no-regrets lifestyle is the exception, not the rule, for most people who haven't received the gift of a chronic illness. I've been living inside the cancer ecosystem for five years. While I hate the physical hammering of chemo, it's the spiritual reset I continually need to remind me to really live, to not take a single day for granted.

Most people live life with the unexpressed intent to arrive unscathed at death. Cancer has taught me that I want to enter heaven used up. The way I see it, there's no better way to live. And the dying part? Well, I look at it this way:

> *I have what is good for me. I shall live on earth till my work is done and not a moment longer. I shall be taken when I'm ripe for heaven and not a minute before. All the powers of the world cannot take away my life until God permits. All the physicians of earth cannot preserve it when God calls me away. J. C. Rile*[24]

A MATTER OF LIFE AND DEATH

Over the last few years, friends have asked me to encourage others who are wrestling with cancer. Two individuals stand out. One was agnostic, the other atheist. Both men were approaching their final days on earth. And both were angry. While I believe it's important to encourage people, it is a matter of life and death to share the importance of faith in Jesus and ultimately his love for them.

Before I spoke to each of those dying men, I felt drawn to the book *No Wonder They Call Him the Savior* by Max Lucado, and more specifically the chapter, "The Tale of the Crucified Crook." It addresses the story of Jesus and the two criminals crucified with him. One of them hurled insults, spewing venom until his dying breath. The other watched as Jesus gasped for air. Most likely that crook had never even said the word *grace*, much less asked for it, but in Jesus, he saw something he had never observed in another man.

Something, though, told him he had never been in better company. And somehow, he realized that even though all he had was prayer, he finally met the One to whom he should pray.

*'Any chance that you could put in a good
word for me?' (Loose translation.)*

'Consider it done.'[25]

Consider it done. What a promise! What an act of
generosity! What grace! Lucado ended the chapter
this way:

> *And it also makes me smile to think there is
> a grinning ex-con walking the golden streets
> who knows more about grace than a thou-
> sand theologians. No one would have given
> him a prayer. But in the end, that is all he
> had. And in the end, that is all it took.*[26]

Like the criminal in Lucado's story, those two
men I spoke with had nothing to offer Jesus. They
were sick, approaching the end of life. They weren't
wealthy, nor could they give back in any significant
way. They had nothing to offer in return for God's
grace and eternal salvation.

I wish I could say those two men heard the
story of the amazing grace Jesus offers and made
deathbed confessions of faith, giving their lives to
the Creator of the Universe, securing their eternity
with him. But they didn't. A friend of one of the

men later told me, "The last few weeks of John's life were complicated, filled with pain and anxiety."

Compare that statement to the account of the passing of 39-year-old Dietrich Bonhoeffer, theologian, and opponent of Nazism, whose last words before his execution on April 8, 1945, were, "This is the end. For me, the beginning of life." [27]

> *A camp doctor who witnessed Bonhoeffer's hanging described the scene: 'Through the half-open door in one room of the huts, I saw Pastor Bonhoeffer, before taking off his prison garb, kneeling on the floor praying fervently to his God. I was most deeply moved by the way this lovable man prayed, so devout and so certain that God heard his prayer. At the place of execution, he again said a prayer and then climbed the steps to the gallows, brave and composed. His death ensued in a few seconds. In the almost 50 years that I have worked as a doctor, I have hardly ever seen a man die so entirely submissive to the will of God.'*[28]

Numerous times over the last few years, I've heard or read about those who embraced death with a strong faith in Jesus. In each instance, these people left this world without anxiety or fear. They had peace on earth because they had the hope of eternity in their hearts.

I believe in heaven, but with everything in me, I also believe that if all believing in Jesus

They had peace on earth because they had the hope of eternity in their hearts.

offers is a better life on earth and peace when my time is up, then that's worth the price of admission. To me, heaven is the bonus.

SOMETHING TO CELEBRATE

Tracey and I had the honor of attending the 2017 National Prayer Breakfast in Washington, D. C., during which Bart Millard, lead singer of the group MercyMe, sang "I Can Only Imagine." Before singing, Bart shared the story of the genesis of this double-platinum hit song.

"I Can Only Imagine" was written after my father passed away with cancer many years ago. He was abusive most of my life. If he had a bad day, he took it out on me. He was diagnosed with cancer when I was a freshman in high school. For me, it was a blessing and a curse. I was kind of glad because I thought (the beatings) would come to an end. But, at the same time, my parents

divorced when I was three. I lived with my
dad most of my life so, he was still my dad
and it was all that I knew. . . . For the next
four or five years, I saw Jesus change him
completely. He went from a monster to being
a man who was desperately and passionately
in love with Jesus. It kind of set me on this
war path for the gospel because, if the gospel
can change that dude, the gospel can change
anybody.[29]

As Bart sang "I Can Only Imagine," I sat among 4,000 other guests with tears streaming down my face. Because of the blessing of cancer, Bart's dad found Christ, left behind his ugly past, *really lived* for five years, and now resides in a place so stunning it surely renders every new entrant speechless. That's something to celebrate. That's the miracle of Jesus. That's embracing interruption all the way to heaven.

LAST WISHES

A few years ago, the wife of a friend of mine walked into her kitchen to prepare a meal. She had no way of knowing a few minutes later she would be wheeled out on a stretcher after suffering an aneurysm. Within hours, her family had to make the difficult decision to remove her from life support. We are simply not promised tomorrow.

The woman's funeral was held in a dark, windowless church. In the lobby, tables held coffee, cookies, and Kool-Aid. One of the women who spoke at the funeral explained her friend had led her to faith in Jesus during their college years. The speaker's parents chose to follow Jesus because of their daughter's newfound faith, as did her husband. Finally, she shared her friend's faithfulness forever changed the lives of her four children.

I sat in that dark, windowless church and wondered, *Why in the heck are we sitting in the dark when this woman brought such light into the world around her? She lived a life worth celebrating!* To me, the passing of that woman from Hotel Earth to heaven was a great excuse for a party. When Jesus participated in a party, he turned water into wine. Guests rolled back the rugs and celebrated for days on end. I'm confident they did not sit!

When I exhale my last bit of carbon dioxide and leave behind my beat-up body, I'll inhale the pure breath of heaven. I like to imagine I'll be in party mode, toasting heaven's other residents with wine reflective of the vintage Jesus produced in his first recorded miracle for the wedding party in Cana in Galilee—saving the best for last. Since I'm going to be in such a magical place with my Savior, Jesus Christ, I want those temporarily left behind on earth to also enjoy a laughter-filled party, not a church service filled with people dressed in black, sitting in a dark room, soaking boxes of scratchy tissues with tears.

One night, soon after that woman's funeral, I couldn't sleep, so I got up and drafted a blog post explaining what I want to occur on the day of my exit party. Here's that post.

September 26, 2014
My Exit Party

I've attended numerous memorial services. Each was quiet, respectful, somber and safe. Most of these affairs have been topped off with coffee, cookies, and Kool-Aid.

Please do not think I'm morbid. Today, I feel terrific. Frankly, I expect to be here for years to come. Really, I do. I simply want to establish my desires for my exit party for when I do make the transition from this earth to the presence of Jesus.

First, I do not want my service in a church building. What is the church? Someone wise once said, "The church is where two people are together, and they are praying for one another . . . That is the church . . . And where the church is, no one is lonely." I love that description!

With that said, please celebrate in a place that fosters conversation, where people lift prayers, and who knows, maybe a few people will experience this brilliant definition of *church*.

In a perfect world, I envision:

- an open field
- a fire pit
- a great meal
- a microphone for friends who want to share fun stories
- great music from Tim Akers & the Smoking Section and a song by my friends Regie Hamm, David White, and Nicole Smith Sponberg
- simple grace-filled messages on the crazy love of Jesus Christ, delivered by my brother Zac and my friend Todd Wagner
- my friends consuming the best wine you can imagine. (Peter Nelson, you're in charge of this.)

- great beer iced in metal tubs (David Caperton, this will be your job.)
- nametags that include where you're from and how you met me
- No coffin. This whole thing should be a celebration of life, not a viewing of death.
- No flowers. Give those bucks to charities like the Both Hands Foundation and Empart USA.

I would prefer a party, a celebration—a time to share the love of Jesus with everyone who joins my family to celebrate my homecoming. I want this to be fun.

It makes me a bit sad to think I won't be there. But something tells me I'll get to watch. It does make me sad to think Tracey will be alone and Jackson will no longer have a dad on earth. These realities give me the courage, desire, and strength to fight this cancer battle for as long as I'm physically able.

When the time does come, please promise me one thing for certain: no coffee, cookies, or Kool-Aid.

AN EPIC WIN

I'm thankful God used cancer to save me from myself. Cancer has sculpted me into someone who understands more deeply, hurts more often, appreciates more quickly, cries more easily, hopes more desperately, loves more openly, and lives more passionately. Frankly, I've discovered life is richer because of my interruption than it was without it. It leads me to places where there are people who need to receive what I can share. It forces me to slow down and make eye contact with God. It makes me solely dependent upon him, and there's not a better place to be.

> I'm thankful God used cancer to save me from myself. I've discovered life is richer because of my interruption than it was without it.

Recently, I read this compelling quote by Atul Gawande in his review of Paul Kalanithi's groundbreaking book *When Breath Becomes Air*: "The dying are the ones who have the most to teach us about life."[30]

I couldn't agree more. God has allowed me—a man with a weak heart, Stage IV cancer, and the attention span of a goldfish—to finish this book about what suffering has taught me. That's something to celebrate. That's the miracle of Jesus. He is allowing me to celebrate out-of-the-blue interruption all the way to heaven, and that's the greatest blessing of all.

I've discovered magic happens through weakness, through suffering, through tears, and when I am forced to cry out. True connection comes through pain, so I'm inclined to ask people to stop praying for my healing. Yes, a better prayer would be for God to glorify himself in my weakness. I believe this is closer to God's heart, and if we're honest with one another, the power of prayer is when it changes our hearts to be closer to his, not the other way around. He is God. He knows better. *Out of the Blue* is his story, not mine. His power is made perfect in my weakness, and that's a good thing.

We aren't meant to live life covered in bubble wrap. There will be bumps and bruises, but I challenge you to trust Jesus and go for it. The great philosopher Rocky Balboa put it this way:

Let me tell you something you already know. The world ain't all sunshine and rainbows. It is a very mean and nasty place and I don't care how tough you are, it will beat you to

That's something to celebrate. That's the miracle of Jesus. He is allowing me to celebrate out-of-the-blue-interruption all the way to heaven, and that's the greatest blessing of all.

your knees and keep you there permanently,
if you let it. You, me, or nobody is going to
hit as hard as life. But it ain't about how
hard you hit; it is about how hard you can
get hit and keep moving forward. How much
you can take and keep moving forward.
That's how winning is done! [31]

If you know Jesus and have placed your faith in him, there's no loss. Passing to the next life is an epic win. When I check out of Hotel Earth, please don't say, "Greg lost his battle with cancer." That will not be the truth. No, when that time comes, when I move to the front of the line, it will be a point in time when I have never been more alive.

> When I check out of Hotel Earth, please don't say, "Greg lost his battle with cancer." That will not be the truth.

It's my desire to make the most of every moment I have left—to squeeze the last drop out of the life I have on this earth. I want to collect experiences, not stuff. Make friends, not deals. Share Jesus and his love with deeds and with words, if necessary. Most of all, I want to arrive in heaven all used up, skidding in broadside with a big "Wow!" and a huge "Yay, God!"

Will you join me?

October 10, 2015
I'm Not Worried, Dad

Last night, on the way home from a Ben Rector concert, 13-year-old Jackson said, "Mr. Mark is nice. This afternoon he called and asked if I was doing ok with your diagnosis." (Mark Stisser is a longtime friend of our family.)

I leaned into the conversation and asked, "Well, are you, Jackson?"

Without skipping a beat, Jackson said, "Dad, while we are praying for your healing, we need to realize our prayers may not be answered that way and, if they're not, it doesn't matter. When you die, you will immediately be with Jesus and, to be honest with you, Mom and I will not be far behind. So, no Dad, I'm not worried."

Last night's concert and conversation were wins on many levels. And for that, I am thankful.

Greg

So, what does this have to do with you?

1. *When life is all said and done, what would an epic win look like for you?*

2. *What do you want your memorial service to look like?*

3. *What would you have to give up to arrive in heaven all used up, skidding in broadside with a big "Wow!" and a huge "Yay, God!"?*

EPILOGUE

BY REGGIE HAMM

"I'm in your garage," is the last text I have from Greg. I keep reading it over and over. There's something surreal about an active text thread from someone who is no longer alive. But I keep reading it. And I can hear him say it in my mind.

Greg was in my garage, standing at my office door, waiting to have a meeting with my friend, Tim Akers. Tim is one of the best musicians in the world and heads a band called the Smoking Section—full of several of the best musicians in the world. Their shows are legendary in Nashville. And A-list artists love to sit in with them.

When you see a Smoking Section show, you never know when Michael McDonald, Vince Gill, or someone like that is going to show up. It's one of the coolest perks of living in Nashville. Tim just happens to be one of my best friends, and I was connecting him with another of my best friends for a strange meeting.

Greg Murtha lived three doors down from me for several years. And he (along with the rest of the neighborhood) watched us turn an old ranch house (that hadn't been touched since it was built in 1973) into a custom home for a special-needs child. Greg didn't know that was what we were doing in there. But he was the only neighbor who would constantly stop and comment on our progress.

"Reg, it's looking great, man!" he yelled from his car one day. And I was a bit taken aback because I wasn't sure how he knew my name. Greg's son Jackson would come over and ask if my daughter could come out to play, when they were small. There was no easy way to explain to him why she couldn't. And we always felt for little Jackson. He so wanted to play with our daughter. But through the sheer will of continually knocking on our door, the entire Murtha family became our friends.

When my book came out, Greg insisted on reading it as soon as possible. And after he read it, he insisted on barging further and further into my life—and I'm so thankful he did. We became very close. He told me once why my book impacted him so much. He said, "Reg, I think some of us in the neighborhood used to think you guys were just anti-social people who were over-protective of your daughter. After reading your book, I realized what was happening in your house was completely the opposite of my perception. You guys were going through hell in there. And I was in walking distance, not knowing it."

For the next several years, Greg would occasionally order an entire box of books from me and hand them out to people randomly. His big take-away was that you can be standing right next to someone and have no idea of what they're going through. He wanted people to think about that.

If Greg Murtha got a single epiphany from my story, I got many from his life. Greg went on to sit on the board of directors of my foundation, Angel Wings. And in every board meeting or planning session, he was the one challenging us to think bigger. He was always asking the important questions. And he was genuinely curious about the answers.

I heard him say on more than one occasion, "when and if we talk to the president about this." And I would interrupt and say, "the president of what, Greg?" His answer? "The president of the United States. Is this important or not?" That attitude made me rethink pretty much everything I do.

Greg traveled the world and worked for organizations that made a difference in people's lives. I think we all aggregate our own personalities with the personalities of others. In my case, I have consciously added a lot of Greg Murtha into my interaction with people. To Greg, no one was unimportant. No one's story was boring. No moment was insignificant. Everything mattered, and every action was a supreme opportunity to show love to someone or to speak it into a situation.

And so, the meeting in my office.

Greg wanted to meet Tim Akers and hire the Smoking Section to play at his memorial service. He told us the story of a funeral he'd recently attended where the deceased had been an amazing woman. She had connected people all over the world and spoken love into people's lives. And at the reception, after the service, they were serving Kool-Aid and cookies and playing somber music.

In Greg's own words, "That really pissed me off." His thought was that her service should have been a huge celebration of a life well-lived. He couldn't get his extraordinary mind around allowing a person of that much significance to be laid to rest in such somber tones.

So, Greg spent the last few months of his life planning his own memorial celebration. And he said he wanted the "best band in Nashville" to play it. He didn't want anyone wearing black or having to endure "horrible organ music" (again, his words). He wanted a lot of people who didn't know each other to show up and meet, drink great wine, eat great food, and dance to great grooves.

We sat in my office and made the plans. And as awkward as it started (for US—it was NEVER awkward for Greg), it ended with smiles and hugs. And after he left, Tim and I talked about what a great idea it was to have this kind of a celebration.

Greg fought through 75 rounds of chemo until his body was simply unable to walk another step. And when my wife kissed him on the head to say goodbye that night, he was still trying to open his eyes and tell us all something. We left the hospital, and Greg was gone two hours later.

I've cried a lot. I'm sure I will cry more. But what I learned from Greg outweighs the sadness. Every time I hear someone say something about his or her life that they think is a minor detail, I say, "Tell me more about that." I learned that from Greg. I wouldn't have come up with that on my own. When people writhe with anger over religion or politics or something they perceive to be injustice, I try to take a step back and ask more questions, instead of meeting them head-on with more anger. God knows I learned that from Greg, and I'm still learning it.

I'm learning that the best life is one of service—NOT ambition and self-focus. And I learned a lot of that from Greg as well.

I don't know how Greg knew this life wisdom at such a young age. But he will be indelibly marked in my heart and on my life. His easy smile and eagerness to serve people are things I will miss. But his inability to end a conversation without telling "just ONE more story, and I'll let you go" is what I will miss the most. Whenever I hear someone say, "last, but not least," I'll think of Greg—and smile.

People from all over the world, from all walks of life, will be at Greg's memorial celebration. And I don't know where he'll be. Some people hope the loved one is looking down. I tend to hope they have moved on to something so dazzling they wouldn't WANT to look down.

Either way, Greg, at YOUR celebration there will be NO Kool-Aid or cookies.

R

ACKNOWLEDGMENTS

Gregory Scott Murtha "moved to the front of the line" at 10:49 p.m. on June 22, 2017. He completed *Out of the Blue* at 8:37 p.m. on June 19, 2017, in room 8637 of Vanderbilt University Medical Center's Critical Care Unit—except for this acknowledgments page.

I had the privilege of spending many hours with Greg talking about this book. For the last year, he called me two or three times a day—and several times a day for the 12 years before that. For those of you who knew Greg, think about how many times I've heard, "one last thing," or "the last thing, I promise," or "promise, I'll let you go after this." Every story was great. Every bit of encouragement blew wind into my sails. Every part of my being misses him today while every part of my soul is thrilled for my brother who is face-to-face with his Savior.

If Greg were writing this acknowledgments page, I'm confident that after long conversations about these things, he would want this section of *Out of the Blue* to read something like the following. I hope I served you well here, my brother.

Alongside, Derek Bell

Tracey, we lived the adventure well. Thank you for being on the journey with me. Your patience and love were evident to everyone as you supported me in all my endeavors for the past 23 years and as you took me to so many hospitals so many times and researched countless natural cancer remedies night after night, year after year. I didn't deserve you, and yet you were by my side to the very end. I could not ask for a better partner in life than you, Tracey.

Jackson, I hope we have prepared you well for the opportunity at life you have before you. You are truly a gift to your mother and me. Always be confident that I love you more than you will ever know. You have been a constant source of pride and joy in my life.

Kelli, you picked up your life and moved to help take care of me. You showed me how the gospel is played out in real time. Everyone should be blessed with an older sister like you.

Zac, we have talked every day on the phone because I love you and I like you. I love you because you are my brother. I like you because you are a great, smart, interesting man—a man of God. Thank you for allowing me to be your big brother.

Dad and Vicki, boy, did our relationship end on a high note! Thank you for being an integral part of my life and formation. I love you, Dad. Vicki, as I said in Room 8637, "You are part of us." Thank you for joining the Murtha Clan.

Mallie Murtha, at some point, everyone will be at the front of the line, and when that time comes, I can't wait to introduce them to you, Mom.

And the Caperton Clan, thank you for loving me even though there were times I acted like a typical son/brother-in-law. It fills my heart knowing that Tracey and Jackson will have you. Love them well.

Ivey Beckman Harrington, this book would have never come to life if it were not for you. I can't thank you enough for working alongside me this last year. It's just like God to pair two limping people together to do something for him. You, with only one working eye, and me, with cancer and a weak heart. What a team!

Robert Lewis, your encouragement about the book and your editorial consulting went a long way in shaping the final manuscript.

Matt Frazier, thank you for pursuing me and gifting me the opportunity to be a part of what we are doing. You are a good and talented man.

Jay Smith, you absolutely capture me through design. Thank you for doing tremendous work on such short notice.

Todd Wagner and Darren Tyler, you guys make Christ's church more radiant. Heaven will be full of men, women, boys, and girls whom you have influenced greatly.

The Leading with a Limp Board of Directors, your encouragement and direction have kept me on the path. Kay, Callie, Michael, Chris, Gary, and Derek—I love you. And to our financial partners (you know who you are), I hope you realize that this book would not have come to fruition without your support. Thank you.

David Seibert and Clear Day Media, I am genuinely excited about our publishing partnership, and I pray that the partnership around *Out of the Blue* takes us on a grand adventure. Let's go big or go home!

Lloyd Reeb and *Bob Buford*, You two believed in me, loved me, put up with me, and encouraged me in my walk with Jesus. You have been the best mentors and friends a guy could hope for.

Ray Gary, you went way beyond servanthood for me and my family while I was sick and working at iDonate. Thank you.

Tracy Noble, you used your gifting to help us polish *Out of the Blue*. Thank you for your attention to detail.

The medical staffs at Vanderbilt University Medical Center, Texas Oncology, at Baylor, MD Anderson, your expertise, compassion, and care are world class.

The patients I met on this journey, thank you for inspiring me to say *yes* to the promptings of the Holy Spirit and for allowing me to be vulnerable and briefly enter your journey. Praying and engaging with you brought me life.

My many friends who read parts of this book and gave me feedback and encouragement. Thank you. Your input is golden.

To those friends who came to the hospital on one of my many trips—thank you. To those who have prayed, cleaned our home, brought meals, hired tree guys to clean up our yard, taken Jackson shopping and to dinner and movies, given our family adventures around the world, and done countless things that happen when the church acts as Christ intended—thank you. You have been the hands and feet of Jesus to my family and me.

I am a grateful man.

To learn more about the life and legacy of Greg Murtha and receive updates about his ministry, visit *{gregmurtha.com.}*

Greg's passion for life is rivaled only by his generosity. If you relish supporting dynamic ministry, here are three organizations Greg invested in and deeply loved.

LEAD**ING** WITH A **LIMP**

Greg launched Leading with a Limp in 2016 to help him spread the "Yes, God, I'm in!" message while battling cancer and living life to the fullest. Greg believes our utmost source of service often springs from our greatest weakness, the place of our deepest pain—and the place where we've suffered is where we have the most to give. Leading with a Limp continues to champion that perspective, and its ministry impacts many lives. Leading with a Limp is a registered 501c3.

LEARN MORE AT
LEADINGWITHALIMP.ORG

The purpose of Both Hands is to help Christian adoptive families fund adoptions by coordinating service projects repairing the homes of widows. At the time of this printing, Both Hands had raised more than eight million dollars for adoptive families, brought 831 orphans closer to home, served 768 widows, and completed more than 700 projects in 42 states.

The vision of Both Hands is to see the day when finances are not an obstacle for Christian families led to adopt, while simultaneously serving every widow in need of home repairs.

LEARN MORE AT
BOTHHANDS.ORG

USA | Empowering & Partnering

To partner with Empart is to play a role in the transformation of hundreds of thousands of lives in South Asia through abolishing spiritual poverty, rescuing children, defending dignity, and providing sustainable solutions. With the goal of transforming 100,000 communities, Empart currently has a presence in more than 22,000 communities.

LEARN MORE AT
EMPARTUSA.ORG

NOTES

A Note from Greg

[1] Sheldon Vanauken, *A Severe Mercy* (New York: HarperCollins Publishers, 1977), 85.

[2] Hunter S. Thompson, http://www.whizzpast.com/20-greatest-hunter-s-thompson-quotes-voted-goodreads/journey to the grave/accessed July 3, 2017.

Chapter 1: Life Interrupted

[3] Bob Goff (@bobgoff). "God's more interested in our hearts than our plans." 7:44 AM – 6 Dec 2014 Tweet, https://twitter.com/bobgoff/status/541256810251173888.

Chapter 2: In the Panic Seat

[4] Charles Duhigg, "How Rick Warren Harnessed the Power of Social Habits and why—after plunging into depression–Saddleback's pastor now pushes spiritual habits through 'The Power of Habit' concept" *Christianity Today*/August 12, 2012.

[5] Bill Hybels, *Simplify: Ten Practices to Unclutter Your Soul* (Carol Stream, IL: Tyndale House Publishers, 2014), 147.

Chapter 3: I Never Saw Sick People

[6] Ann Voskamp, *The Broken Way: A Daring Path into the Abundant Life* (Grand Rapids: Zondervan, 2016), 175.

[7] Job 2:9 NIV.

[8] J. C. Ryle, *Matthew: Expository Thoughts on the Gospels* (Wheaton: Crossway, 1993), 130-131.

Chapter 4: Everyone is Broken

[9] Ann Voskamp, *The Broken Way: A Daring Path into the Abundant Life* (Grand Rapids: Zondervan, 2016), 185, 186.

[10] Ibid, 185, 186.

Chapter 5: God's Math

[11] Hank Williams, *I Saw the Light*, Marc Abraham writer and director. (Sony Pictures, 2016), Film.

[12] Thomas Merton and Lawrence S. Cunningham. *Thomas Merton: Spiritual Master: The Essential Writings.* (New York: Paulist, 1992), 364-365.

Chapter 7: What's in Your Bucket?

[13] Howard Thurman Center for Common Ground, https://www.bu.edu/thurman/about/history.

Chapter 8: Investing in My Son

[14] Mark Twain. "50 Best Inspiring Mark Twain Quotes About Life," http://quotesideas.com/marktwain.

[15] Bob Goff, *Love Does*, (Nashville: Thomas Nelson, 2012), 224.

Chapter 10: Church of the Bent and Bruised

[16] Groucho Marx, *Groucho and Me*, "Groucho Marx's letter of resignation to the Friars' Club," (Da Capo Press Inc., New York, 1995 [reprint of 1959 edition], 321.

[17] Brennan Manning, *The Ragamuffin Gospel* (New York: Penguin Random House, 2005), "A Word Before."

[18] Ibid.

[19] Denison Forum. May 4, 2017.

[20] *Christianity Today*, Christian History, "Dietrich Bonhoeffer: German Theologian and Resister," http://www.christianitytoday.com/history/people/martyrs/dietrich-bonhoeffer.html.

Chapter 11: The Adventure of Yes

21 Katie Davis, *Kisses from Katie: A Story of Relentless Love and Redemption*, (New York: Howard Books, 2011), xix.

22 Katie Davis, *Kisses from Katie: A Story of Relentless Love and Redemption*, (New York: Howard Books, 2011), xi.

Chapter 12: My Final Chapter

23 William Wallace, *Braveheart*, Director Mel Gibson, Writer Randall Wallace, (Paramount, 1995), Film.

24 J. C. Rile, *Expository Thoughts on the Gospels*, (London: Steam Press), 139.

25 Max Lucado, *No Wonder They Call Him the Savior*, (Nashville: Thomas Nelson, 2011), 17.

26 Ibid, 18.

27 Clyde E. Fant, and Dietrich Bonhoeffer. B*onhoeffer: Worldly Preaching*, (Nashville: T. Nelson, 1975), 24.

28 *Christianity Today*, Christian History, "Dietrich Bonhoeffer: German Theologian and Resister," http://www.christianityto-day.com/history/people/martyrs/dietrich-bonhoeffer.html.

29 Bart Millard, "I Can Only Imagine." Story transcript from 2017 National Prayer Breakfast, Washington, D.C.

30 Kellyn Loehr, "Atul Gawande." Paul Kalanithi, 26 Mar. 2016. Web. 03 July 2017, http://paulkalanithi.com/news-source.

31 Sylvester Stallone, *Rocky Balboa*, Director, writer, producer Sylvester Stallone, (Columbia, 2006), Film.